Beginner's Guide to
LOCOMOTIVES &
ROLLING STOCK

Cody Grivno

KALMBACH BOOKS

WAUKESHA, WI

Dedication

This book is dedicated to my wife, Dorothy. Thanks for your love, encouragement, and understanding on the many nights when I'd come home from a full day at *Model Railroader*, have a quick meal with you and the kids, and head into the office to work on this book into the early hours of the morning. You're an amazing wife and mother. I'm truly blessed.

Acknowledgements

The *Beginner's Guide to Locomotives and Freight Cars* was written for entry-level and intermediate modelers in N and HO scales. Some of the topics in this book have been covered many times before in the hobby press and books, while other topics are being covered for the first time. I hope the tips and techniques in this book will add to your enjoyment of model railroading, the world's greatest hobby.

There are many people that deserve credit for making this book happen. First, my friends at Kalmbach Books.

Thanks to Dianne Wheeler for giving this project the green light, Jeff Wilson for contributing the prototype steam locomotive chapter, Randy Rehberg for answering my questions, and Tom Ford for turning the words and pictures into the product you're holding in your hands.

I'd also like to thank the manufacturers who contributed supplies that helped make this book complete: Debra Schiff (Bachmann Trains), Matt Gaudynski (Fox Valley Models), Ben Thielemann (Micro-Trains Line Co.), Pat Sanders (Trainworx), and Lance Burton and Kara Yanacheck (Wm. K. Walthers Inc.).

Last, but by no means least, I owe a big thank you to my coworkers at *Model Railroader*. Thanks for asking how the project was going, for your encouraging words, and for your ideas. It's a blessing to work with such an enthusiastic group of modelers.

Cody Grivno
Slinger, Wis.
September 2016

Kalmbach Books
21027 Crossroads Circle
Waukesha, Wisconsin 53186
www.KalmbachHobbyStore.com

Published in 2017
21 20 19 18 17   1 2 3 4 5

Manufactured in China

ISBN: 978-1-62700-299-8
EISBN: 978-1-62700-300-1

Editor: Jeff Wilson
Book Design: Tom Ford

Library of Congress Control Number: 2016943719

Contents

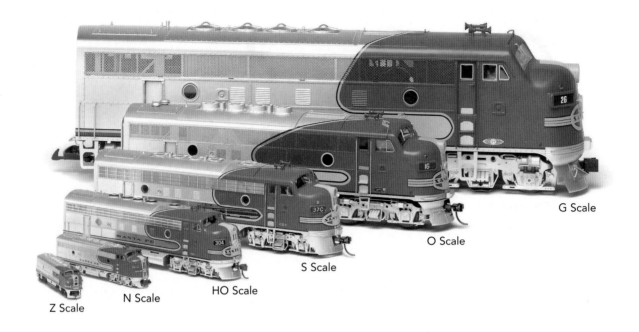

CHAPTER ONE

Getting started

The above photo shows a comparison of the popular modeling scales. From left are Z (1:220), N (1:160), HO (1:87.1), S (1:64), O (1:48), and G.
Bill Zuback

There are many ways to get into model railroading. The typical path involves receiving a train set for a birthday or at Christmas. Others are exposed to the hobby by seeing a layout at a model railroad club, a train show, or a neighbor's house. Some may even become interested in model trains because a family member or friend is a professional railroader. Regardless of how you discovered the hobby, welcome to model railroading!

This ready-to-run Blackstone Models HOn3 Denver & Rio Grande Western K-27 2-8-2 steam locomotive is an example of the fine narrow gauge models offered today. *Bill Zuback*

The locomotives and freight cars on Dan Sylvester's highly detailed HOn3 Rio Grande Southern may be narrow gauge, but the surrounding structures, vehicles, and figures are HO scale.

Scale versus gauge

As you get started in model railroading, you may hear people use the terms "scale" and "gauge." Unfortunately, some people use the terms interchangeably, which can lead to confusion.

Scale is the proportion of the model to the prototype. In this book, we'll focus on HO (1:87.1) and N (1:160) scales. Other popular modeling scales include Z (1:220), S (1:64), O (1:48), and large (1:32 to 1:20), **1**.

Gauge is the distance between the railheads on track. On prototype railroads in North America, the standard track gauge is 4'-8½".

Rails on narrow gauge lines are closer together. Famous three-foot-gauge lines include the Denver & Rio Grande Western and Rio Grande Southern in Colorado, the White Pass & Yukon in Alaska, and the East Broad Top in Pennsylvania. The Sandy River & Rangeley Lakes was a noted two-foot-gauge line in Maine.

Narrow gauge modeling has become

4

Moloco's HO scale General American 50-foot insulated boxcar is an example of the high-end plastic models available today. It features many separately applied, prototype-specific detail parts. *Bill Zuback*

5

HO scale models are approximately half the size of O scale models, hence the name HO. The O scale Trinity 5,161-cubic-foot-capacity covered hopper is from Atlas O. The HO version in the foreground is from Athearn.

6

These HO scale models show examples of what is on the market today. From left to right are a Tangent Scale Models four-bay hopper with many separately applied parts, a mid-level InterMountain Value Line 14-panel Johnstown America Coalporter gondola with some separate parts, and a WalthersTrainline offset-side four-bay hopper with mainly molded-on details.

a popular aspect of the hobby, thanks in part to the availability of quality models from Bachmann, Blackstone Models, and others, **2**. Narrow gauge models are indicated by a lower case "n" after the scale, such as HOn3. While the equipment and track is three-foot gauge, the vehicles and structures on the layout should still be HO scale, **3**.

Getting to know HO scale

The most popular modeling scale today is HO scale, pronounced "aitch oh." Models in HO are 1:87.1 proportion, meaning each dimension is $\frac{1}{87}$ as long as the prototype, **4**. (To modelers, "prototype" refers to real, full-size trains, structures, and other items.)

The name HO scale was derived because the models are approximately half the size of O scale models, **5**. Though the scale dates back to the Great Depression of the 1930s, HO came of age after World War II and quickly surpassed O scale in popularity.

Today, about 80 percent of hobbyists model in HO scale. Not surprisingly, the greatest product variety can be found in the scale. Most major diesel locomotives have been produced in HO, as have many steam locomotives, freight cars, structures, and detail parts, **6**.

The variety is further reflected by the size of the annual HO scale reference book produced by Wm. K. Walthers, Inc., a Milwaukee, Wis.-based model railroad manufacturer and distributor. The 2016 edition was in excess of 1,000 pages.

The world of N scale

N scale traces its roots to the 1960s. The models in N scale are 1:160 proportion, or 160 times smaller than full-size railroad equipment, **7**.

The scale first gained popularity in Europe, where its small size appealed to those living in compact spaces. The scale's name was derived from the 9mm rail gauge, as nine starts with "n" in some European languages.

Though N scale was in the United States during the 1960s and '70s, the early models were crude by today's standards. Locomotives and freight cars often had oversized details and wheel flanges, Rapido couplers were the norm, the track looked bulky, and locomotive performance was sketchy at best.

N scale began appearing regularly in the hobby press in the early 1970s. At the end of that decade, *Model Railroader* magazine's Clinchfield project layout played a big role in bringing N scale into the mainstream, **8**. From the 1980s onward, N scale models have improved dramatically in quality and quantity, **9**. Approximately 20 percent of modelers are in N scale, per *Model Railroader* surveys.

N scale models are approximately half the size of those in HO, **10**. Much of N scale's popularity can be attributed to that size difference. A nice-sized layout can fit into an apartment or spare bedroom. If space isn't at a premium, vast stretches of right-of-way can be modeled between towns. This makes it possible to run long trains without having the locomotive in one town and the caboose in the other, **11**.

Model variety

Many veteran modelers will tell you now is the best time to be in model railroading, and they couldn't be more accurate. The quality and number of models in N and HO scales is better than ever before. But how do you make sense of all the options on the market today?

Though kits aren't as prominent as they were in previous decades, they're still available, **12**. Accurail, Atlas, Bowser, and ScaleTrains.com are among manufacturers that offer kits in HO scale. These easy-to-build models can be completed in an evening, often in less than 30 minutes. Some kits are offered in N scale, but they're not as common.

The bulk of the models on the market today are ready-to-run. Many of the large manufacturers have multiple product lines that cover the gamut of price points, **13**. The budget-priced models currently available are a big step up from those available in prior decades. While some of the paint schemes may not be accurate for the body style, most of the cars have metal wheelsets and body-mounted plastic knuckle couplers, much improved from

7

Micro-Trains has been manufacturing N scale models since the early 1970s. This Southern Pacific bay-window caboose is an example of its modern offerings. *Bill Zuback*

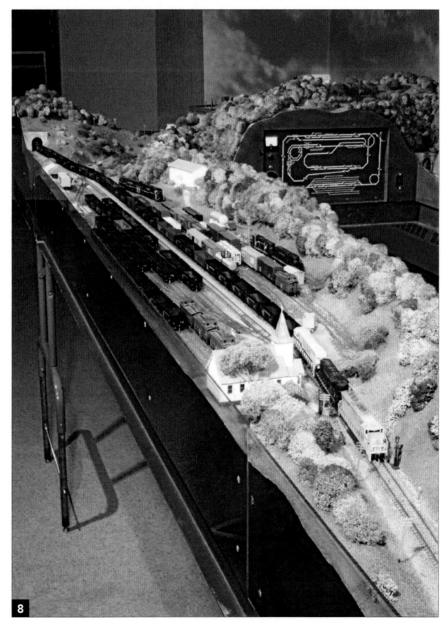

8

Model Railroader magazine's Clinchfield project layout was pivotal in putting N scale on the map. A series of articles in 1978 described its construction. *A.L. Schmidt*

9

This photo shows the evolution of N scale models over the decades, from crudely proportioned, poorly detailed models with Rapido couplers at lower left to the nicely detailed, prototype-specific models with knuckle couplers at right. *Bill Zuback*

10

N scale models are just over half the size of HO scale. The N scale model in the foreground is from ExactRail. The model in the background is from Athearn.

the days of horn-hook (HO) or Rapido (N) couplers and plastic wheelsets **14**.

Mid-level models typically feature some separately applied details, metal wheelsets, and plastic or metal knuckle couplers, **15**. The models are usually offered in two or more road numbers and more closely follow the prototype.

High-end models are exact or near-exact copies of full-size railroad equipment, **16**. In addition to metal wheelsets and knuckle couplers, these models often have etched-metal parts, road-name specific details, and freestanding brake detail. Because these models have fine details, they should be handled with care.

Train sets

Train sets make getting started in model railroading easy. Most contain a locomotive, caboose, a few freight cars, track, a power pack, and perhaps a structure, **17**. As with many aspects of the hobby, you get what you pay for. A cheap set with toy-like equipment probably won't run as well or last as long as a higher-priced set with better looking models.

The big difference is the locomotives. The HO scale Electro-Motive Corp. FT in **18** is from Bachmann's HO scale Santa Fe Flyer train set. These sets are designed for the mass market (i.e. big box stores), so they're

11

Running long trains in a reasonable amount of space is just one of the many appeals of N scale. This scene takes place on Daryl Kruse's 14 x 28-foot Union Pacific Rochelle Subdivision layout. *Daryl Kruse*

not made to the same level of detail as Bachmann's higher-end products. The FT features a light die-cast metal chassis and a basic motor. The plastic body shell features molded details.

The HO scale Electro-Motive Division GP38-2 diesel locomotive in **19** is from Athearn's HO scale Iron Horse Express. It features acetal handrails, drill starter points for adding grab irons and lift rings, a heavy die-cast metal chassis, and a five-pole skew-wound motor used in the company's Ready-to-Roll line of models.

Another major difference in detail and quality is the freight cars, **20**. The Bachmann train-set gondola shown in the photo is unpainted (molded in black plastic) with molded details and has plastic wheelsets.

The do-it-yourself approach

While train sets are a great one-stop way to get up and running, they may not contain the trains and/or track arrangement you're interested in. Most train sets feature equipment from well-known railroads like the Atchison, Topeka & Santa Fe; BNSF Ry.; CSX; New York Central; Pennsylvania RR; and Union Pacific. Why? Those road names sell well, as they're familiar.

If you're looking for equipment painted for regional and short line railroads, you'll need to take a trip to the local hobby shop, **21**. Starting your model railroad piece-by-piece may cost a bit more, but in the end you'll have the railroad you want.

First, look for a reliable ready-to-run locomotive, such as those offered by Athearn, Atlas, Bachmann, Bowser (HO), Broadway Limited Imports, Fox Valley Models, Hornby Hobbies, InterMountain, Kato, Rapido Trains, and Walthers, among others. Unless noted, all of these companies offer locomotives in HO and N scales.

Then look for quality ready-to-run freight cars. Many of the manufacturers listed above make freight cars in HO and N. Other companies that make ready-to-run rolling stock include Bluford Shops (HO and N), Con-Cor (HO and N), DeLuxe Innovations (N), ExactRail (HO and N), Kadee

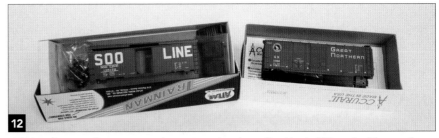

Atlas and Accurail are among the companies that offer kits in HO scale. Kits are fun projects and a great way to develop modeling skills.

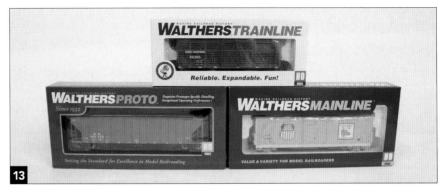

Ready-to-run models are now standard in HO and N scales. Several companies have multiple product lines that cover various price points. WalthersTrainline, WalthersMainline, and WalthersProto are three HO product lines from Walthers.

Budget-priced models have come a long way from previous decades. This Atlas Trainman series HO scale Thrall 4,750-cubic-foot-capacity covered hopper features metal wheels (on plastic axles) and body-mounted knuckle couplers.

These HO Trinity 31,000-gallon tank cars are part of ScaleTrains.com's Operator line. They feature simplified painting and fewer separately applied details. The company also produces high-end versions of the same car with more details. *Bill Zuback*

16

High-end models closely follow the prototypes they're based on. Each of these HO EMD GP9 diesel locomotives, from Athearn's Genesis series, feature details specific to the exact road numbers of the Burlington Northern diesels they represent. *Bill Zuback*

17

This WalthersTrainline HO scale train set features a ready-to-run locomotive, three freight cars, a caboose, and an oval of track. This set also includes a power pack and DVD on how to build your first railroad.

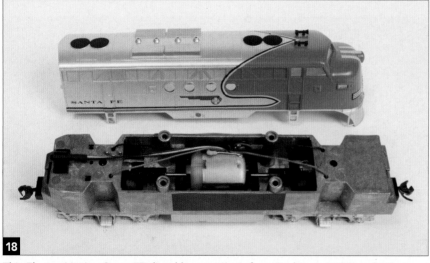

18

This Electro-Motive Corp. FT diesel locomotive is from Bachmann's HO scale Santa Fe Flyer train set. The model features a basic shell with most details molded in place, a light die-cast metal chassis, and basic motor.

(HO), Micro-Trains (N), Tangent Scale Models (HO), and Trainworx (N) **22**.

Next, select track components and a power pack. Track is available from Atlas, Bachmann, Kato, Micro-Engineering, Peco, and Walthers. Except for Walthers, all of the firms offer track in HO and N scale. Atlas and Bachmann offer track with and without molded roadbed; Kato's Unitrack is only available with molded roadbed.

Finally, select a power pack. Model Rectifier Corp. offers a wide variety of control systems for direct current and Digital Command Control (DCC). Atlas, Bachmann, and Kato also offer power packs.

Get started

Model railroading is a fun and rewarding hobby. It's more than just watching trains run in circles. The hobby teaches valuable skills in carpentry, electronics, history, budgeting, and much more.

There's no right or wrong way to enjoy model railroading. Some hobbyists enjoy model building—making structures, locomotives, and freight cars look like their full-size counterparts. Others enjoy running their layout (or those of friends) in a prototypical manner, investing hours of research in employee timetables, rule books, and other publications to learn the ins and outs how their favorite prototype railroad worked on the equipment it ran.

That said, there are a few things to remember if you're new to the hobby. First, learn all you can. *Model Railroader* magazine has been around for more than 80 years and is the world's leading publication on the topic. It features how-to articles on benchwork, wiring, scenery, painting, structure building, among many other topics. The magazine also features the best layouts from around the world, product reviews, and prototype information. You can learn more online at www.ModelRailroader.com.

A sister subscription website, ModelRailroaderVideoPlus.com, features how-to videos, layout visits, information on Digital Command Control, and much more. The website also features project layouts not shown in the magazine, with step-by-step instructions on the construction process.

In addition, Kalmbach Books produces titles like the one you're holding in your hand, as well as books on scenery, wiring, painting, Digital Command Control, and other topics. You can see the entire library of print and digital books at KalmbachHobbyStore.com.

Second, start small. It's easy to see the basement-filling model railroads featured in magazines, books, and online and try to build something similar. This will lead to frustration. Instead, try building something more manageable, like a 4 x 8-foot layout on a piece of plywood or a shelf layout that spans a few bookshelves. These smaller platforms let you learn the various aspects of the hobby in a smaller space.

Third, keep practicing. Develop your skills on basic freight car and structure kits. As your skills grow, so will your confidence to try more advanced kits.

In the following chapters, you'll learn the basics of prototype and model locomotives and freight cars, model maintenance, couplers, trucks, wheels, tools, and glues. I hope this information serves you well.

19 This Electro-Motive Division GP38-2 is from Athearn's Iron Horse Express HO scale set. The model features a five-pole skew-wound motor and heavy, die-cast metal chassis typical of the company's Ready-to-Roll models.

20 Inexpensive train sets designed for mass-market stores often feature basic freight cars. This Bachmann Wabash gondola has an unpainted black plastic body with details molded in place and uses plastic wheelsets.

21 It's not very likely that you'll find locomotives and freight cars for regional and short line railroads or private-car owners in train sets. However, you can find these items at your local hobby shop.

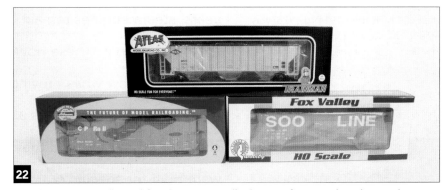

22 Your locomotive will need freight cars to pull. Three or four good-quality ready-to-run models will be a good starting point for your model railroad.

CHAPTER TWO

Prototype
steam locomotives

A Pennsylvania Railroad class K4s Pacific (4-6-2) leads the *Liberty Limited* away from Inglewood Station (Chicago) in February 1940. The Pacific was the most common passenger locomotive of the 1900s, and the Pennsy's K4s (with more than 400 built from 1914 to 1928) was among the most-famous of the type. *Harold Stirton collection*

Steam locomotives ruled North American railroads from the early days of railroading through the 1940s. Even though they've been gone from revenue service for more than 60 years, steam engines remain favorites among modelers for many reasons. These powerful machines provide an impressive show while moving, with the rhythmic motion of valve gear and side rods along with visible and audible chuffs to show how hard they're working. Steam locomotives were built for specific duties and applications, meaning each railroad's engines had a distinct appearance and character.

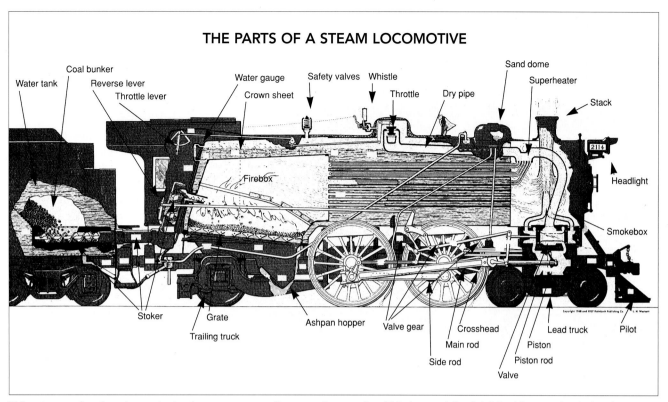

THE PARTS OF A STEAM LOCOMOTIVE

This cutaway drawing shows the basic components of a steam locomotive. This is a coal-fired 4-4-2 with a mechanical stoker.

Models of steam engines, like their prototypes, are fascinating to watch. And, with the tremendous growth in Digital Command Control, sound effects make steam models even more appealing.

Understanding how prototype steam locomotives work, how they evolved, and knowing what kinds of locomotives were used in various types of service will help you better determine which model steam engines are appropriate for your layout. It will also help you to better model them in terms of details, operations, and weathering—all subjects we'll examine more thoroughly in Chapter 3.

How steam locomotives work

The cutaway drawing above shows the basic components of a steam locomotive and illustrates how they work. Follow along with the diagram as we trace the basic construction and operation of a steam engine.

The locomotive rests on several sets of wheels, with small wheels at the front and rear (the lead and trailing trucks) and the large driving wheels ("drivers") in the middle. The number of wheels and their size varies among locomotives based on power and the type of service.

A long, horizontal boiler holds water, which is heated by a fire in a firebox. A series of flues or tubes run through the boiler between the firebox and the smokebox (at the front of the locomotive), providing more surface area for heating the water.

The drawing shows a coal-fired locomotive, the most common type. In the firebox, a brick arch extends from the bottom front above the fire itself, improving combustion and ensuring that the draft doesn't draw the fire and fuel directly out of the firebox through the flues. The burning coal rests on a grate at the base of the firebox; the ashpan or ashpan hopper below it catches ashes as the coal burns.

Coal engines can be hand-fired, meaning the fireman physically scoops coal from the tender through the fire-box door into the firebox. Larger and more modern locomotives had mechanical stokers that carried coal from the tender under the cab floor or deck and up into the firebox. The drawing shows a common auger-style stoker.

Many locomotives—especially on southwestern railroads where oil refineries were nearer than coalfields—burned fuel oil instead of coal. Oil burners relied on jets to atomize the fuel into a spray for burning within the firebox. The fuel was thick—much thicker than common (no. 2) fuel oil today—typically Bunker C (or no. 6 fuel oil). It required preheating (via steam) to flow properly, and the tender tank was slightly pressurized.

The firebox on an oil burner lacked a grate and ashpan. For the fireman, maintaining the fire meant adjusting valves to control the oil flow. Other than that, the basic locomotive operations were the same.

The top surface of the firebox is called the "crown sheet." The water level in the boiler must be kept high enough to cover the crown sheet at all times, or the extreme heat of the firebox will cause the steel sheet to weaken and fail. This leads to a boiler explosion—probably the most-feared danger of steam locomotives.

As the water boils, steam is collected at the top of the boiler in the steam dome. There, a lever from the throttle opens and closes a valve atop the dry pipe, which allows steam to pass to a valve above the cylinders on each side

The drivers are all connected by horizontal side rods. The main rod (at an angle) connects the piston (within the large cylinder casting at right) to the main driver, while the valve gear regulates direction and steam cutoff. *Robert Hale*

This view of a cab interior shows an array of valves, gauges, and controls along the backhead. Below the cab deck is the stoker tube, which will be connected to the tender; the firebox door is just above the deck. *Trains magazine collection*

of the locomotive. In most modern steam locomotives, the steam first passes through a "superheater"—a series of pipes that pass through the boiler flues. This increases the temperature of the steam, making the engine more efficient.

When the cylinder valve opens, it admits steam into the cylinder, the large box or casing located in front of the drivers and directly below the exhaust stack. Within the cylinder, the steam expands, forcing a large piston into motion. The piston travels back and forth in the cylinder, with steam imparting motion in each direction.

The piston is connected to the front of the main rod. The other end of the main rod is connected to a crankpin on the main driving wheel (driver). As the piston moves, it pushes or pulls the main rod, putting the locomotive in motion. Side rods connect the main driver to the remaining drivers, powering all driving axles.

The driver crankpins on opposite sides of a locomotive are positioned at 90 degrees of rotation from each other (called "quartering"). This smoothens the potential pounding action of the side rods and ensures that the locomotive doesn't accidentally stop with both main rods in a dead-center position (evenly in front or behind the wheel center) where no force could be transmitted by the main rod, resulting in a stall.

A collection of rods and linkage called the valve gear controls whether the locomotive goes forward or back-ward and also sets the amount of time the cylinder valve admits steam into the cylinder, called the "cutoff." The valve gear is controlled by the engi-neer using the reversing lever. When set for long cutoff, steam is admitted for a longer time, needed when start-ing a train or pulling a heavy train at low speed. With short cutoff, steam is admitted for a shorter time. Used when at high speed or with lighter loads, short cutoff uses less steam and is more efficient. Think of adjusting cutoff as the steam locomotive equivalent to low and high gears in a truck.

Once the steam has been used in the cylinder, the cylinder valve opens and the steam discharges vertically

A Chicago, St. Paul, Minneapolis & Omaha Mikado (2-8-2) tops off its coal load from a coaling tower in 1954. *Philip R. Hastings*

Whyte locomotive classifications

0-4-0	Four-wheel switcher	<OO
0-6-0	Six-wheel switcher	<OOO
0-8-0	Eight-wheel switcher	<OOOO
0-10-2	Union	<OOOOOo
2-4-2	Columbia	<oOOo
2-6-0	Mogul	<oOOO
2-6-2	Prairie	<oOOOo
2-8-0	Consolidation	<oOOOO
2-8-2	Mikado	<oOOOOo
2-8-4	Berkshire	<oOOOOoo
2-10-0	Decapod	<oOOOOO
2-10-2	Santa Fe	<oOOOOOo
2-10-4	Texas	<oOOOOOoo
2-6-6-6	Allegheny	<oOOO OOO ooo
2-8-8-4	Yellowstone	<oOOOO OOOOoo
4-4-0	American	<ooOO
4-4-2	Atlantic	<ooOOo
4-4-4	Jubilee	<ooOOoo
4-6-0	Ten-Wheeler	<ooOOO
4-6-2	Pacific	<ooOOOo
4-6-4	Hudson	<ooOOOoo
4-8-0	Twelve-Wheeler	<ooOOOO
4-8-2	Mountain	<ooOOOOo
4-8-4	Northern	<ooOOOOoo
4-10-0	Mastadon	<ooOOOOO
4-10-2	Southern Pacific	<ooOOOOOo
4-12-2	Union Pacific	<ooOOOOOOo
4-6-6-4	Challenger	<ooOOO OOOoo
4-8-8-4	Big Boy	<ooOOOO OOOOoo

This Milwaukee Road 4-6-4 is an oil-burner—note the lack of an open coal bunker on the tender. The rear stenciling indicates a capacity of 18,000 gallons of water and 7,000 gallons of oil. *Milwaukee Road*

Locomotive builders

There were dozens of companies building steam locomotives in the 1800s, but as locomotives became larger, small shops gave way to larger locomotive works. By the turn of the 20th century, most locomotives (those not built by individual railroads) were being produced by three major companies: Alco, Baldwin, and Lima.

Baldwin was the largest (and longest-lived) steam builder. The company began in Philadelphia in 1831, and continued producing steam locomotives for railroads across the country until the last Chesapeake & Ohio 2-6-6-2 emerged in 1949. The company continued building diesels, but never had a large share of that market, and was out of business in 1956.

American Locomotive Works (Alco) was formed when eight smaller companies merged in 1901 (with two additional plants joining in 1902 and 1905) in an effort to better compete with Baldwin. The largest of these was Schenectady (N.Y.) Locomotive Works, and that's where all Alco production was moved by 1929. Alco built its last steam locomotive in 1948 but continued building diesels until 1969.

The other major builder was Lima Locomotive Works of Lima, Ohio. The company started in 1869 building Shay (geared) locomotives, then expanded in the early 1900s to produce conventional locomotives. The company's "Super Power" concept drove sales of high-horsepower locomotives in the 1930s through the end of steam production in 1947.

In addition to these builders, many railroads built locomotives in their own shops. The best-known and most prolific were the Pennsylvania RR and the Norfolk & Western, both known for having extensive steam fleets home-built to their own designs. The N&W in 1953 built the last reciprocating steam locomotive for common-carrier service in the country (0-8-0 no. 244).

through the smokebox, up the blast pipe, and out the exhaust stack. This provides the familiar "chuff" sound. The steam discharge creates a draft for the firebox, drawing hot air forward through the flues.

Because of the quartering of the drivers, and that each cylinder provides two power strokes per driver revolution, for a two-cylinder locomotive you'll hear four chuffs for every rotation of the drivers.

The cab provides shelter for the engineer, who sits on the right-hand side, and the fireman, who sits on the left. Most of the controls are on the "backhead," the wall that separates the cab from the firebox and boiler.

The backhead holds a complex array of valves, gauges, and controls, a reminder that steam locomotives are complex machines. The most-used controls include the throttle, reversing lever, and brake stand on the engineer's side. A water-sight glass provides visual confirmation of the boiler's water level, ensuring the crew that the crown sheet is covered. The steam gauge shows how much pressure is being produced. A dropping steam gauge required action to be taken by the fireman; if the pressure became too high, a safety valve atop the boiler released excess pressure.

Most modern steam locomotives had speedometers, but many early locomotives did not, requiring crews to calculate speed with a pocket watch and mile markers.

Other controls include valves to control the mechanical stoker (including steam jets that redirect coal within the firebox), valves controlling the injectors and/or water pump to add water to the boiler, and valves controlling the air compressors, dynamo, steam heat line, water pump, and other accessories.

Tender

The tender is the car immediately behind (and semipermanantly coupled to) the locomotive. You'll sometimes hear it incorrectly called a "coal car." The tender carries both the water supply and fuel (oil or coal) for the locomotive. You can tell what fuel the locomotive burns by looking at the tender: A coal tender has coal in an open-top bunker at the front, with the coal visible. Oil tenders are more streamlined, as the oil and water are both enclosed in tanks.

Tender size and style varied widely by manufacturer and railroad. Tenders are rated in size by both their coal capacity in tons and water (and oil, if used) capacity in gallons. In general, road locomotives had larger tenders than switchers, and the larger the locomotive, the faster it would use both water and fuel, so the larger the tender.

Through the early 1900s, tenders rode on conventional trucks—either four-wheel or six-wheel depending upon size. As locomotives became larger and tender size increased, manufacturers moved to what became known as a centipede design, with several axles along the frame. The middle wheels were allowed to move side to side, allowing them to negotiate curves.

One distinctive variation was the Vanderbilt tender. These had a cylindrical tank visible at the rear, with a squared-off coal bunker at the front. They were lighter compared to standard designs.

Switchers often used slope-back tenders. These had a lower profile, with the rear of the tender sloping downward from the back of the coal bunker. These allowed better visibility to the rear, important for the many reversing moves during switching.

Wheel arrangements

Steam locomotives are categorized by their wheel arrangements, which provide an indication of their size and use. This is known as the Whyte classification system (named for its developer, Frederick Whyte). A list of the most common wheel arrangements is shown in the chart on page 15. To determine the wheel arrangement, count the number of wheels on the lead (pilot) truck, then the number of drivers, then the number of wheels on the trailing truck.

Most wheel arrangements also have names—often related to the first user of a specific model, but sometimes based on region or usage. Some names varied among railroads. For example, the 4-8-4 was first called a Northern, having first appeared on the Northern Pacific. However, railroads in the East and South would have none of that, so the 4-8-4 became known on various railroads as a Dixie, Potomac, Greenbrier, or Niagara.

Pilot trucks support part of the weight of the front of the locomotive and serve to stabilize the ride. They help guide a locomotive into curves, especially at high speeds. Passenger locomotives generally have four-wheel pilot trucks; freight locomotive pilots have two and sometimes four wheels. Switchers generally had no pilot or trailing trucks, which was fine for slow-speed operations.

Trailing trucks were rare until around 1900. As locomotive size increased, fireboxes had to become larger as well. With increased boiler capacity, the firebox was moved back, behind the rear driver, requiring support from a trailing truck. Two-wheel trailing trucks gave way to four-wheel trucks on later locomotives with larger fireboxes.

Evolution and specialization

As steam locomotives evolved, becoming larger and more powerful, this often meant new designs and wheel arrangements. Sometimes existing wheel arrangements were used, but with larger boilers and fireboxes.

This means that not all locomotives of a given wheel arrangement are alike. They differ—often dramatically—in power, speed, and appearance.

Although by 1900 most steam locomotives were being built by three manufacturers (Baldwin, Lima, and Alco), each locomotive order was a custom design. Unlike automobiles and trucks, which would soon become built to standard designs on assembly lines, railroads ordered and builders delivered locomotives designed not just for a specific railroad, but often for a particular purpose, region, or division.

Unlike diesels, steam locomotives were not easily adaptable to multiple uses. Elements of a locomotive's design that made it work well for one type of

Baltimore & Ohio no. 5500, a 4-8-2, has a Vanderbilt tender riding on six-wheel trucks. *Harold K. Vollrath collection*

The 4-4-0 American was a common early locomotive type. This late-1800s Milwaukee Road locomotive has a small boiler and large angled pilot. *Milwaukee Road*

Switching locomotives, like this Pennsylvania 0-4-0, lacked lead and trailing trucks. Small sloped-back tenders were common on switching locomotives.
Bert Pennypacker

The ultimate development of the articulated locomotive was Union Pacific's 4-8-8-4 Big Boy. Articulateds were essentially two engines under a single boiler.
R.F. Collins; collection of Louis A. Marre

The Shay was the most common type of geared locomotive. It had vertical cylinders powering a drive shaft along one side. Western Maryland no. 6 was one of the last ones built, in 1945. *Lima Locomotive Works*

service hindered or made it unusable for another.

Driver size was key: Tall (large-diameter) drivers were suited for high speeds, such as passenger service, but provided low starting tractive effort (needed to get heavy trains rolling). Short (small-diameter) drivers meant high tractive effort at low speeds, good for switching or slow-speed, heavy freights, but limited the top speed, making them unsuitable for fast freight or passenger trains.

Number of drivers, frame length, and weight on drivers was also important. The Union Pacific used long-framed 4-12-2s for fast freights on the straight lines of the Western plains, but railroads traversing

mountains were limited to shorter wheelbase locomotives because of tight curves, and often chose flexible-yet-powerful articulated locomotives.

A single railroad might have multiple types of locomotives for different divisions: One type for fast freight service on flatland areas, another for rolling hills, and yet another for the steep climbs and sharp curves of mountains.

Coal quality was another design factor: The better the coal, the smaller the firebox. Northern Pacific locomotives, for example, relied on poor-quality (but cheap, plentiful, and local) lignite, and required huge fireboxes. Northeastern lines that burned anthracite—a high-quality coal,

but one that burned slowly—required specially designed wide, deep fireboxes.

Other locomotive options affected appearance, including the size and style (and location) of items such as cabs, feedwater heaters, air pumps headlights, bells, number boxes, and whistles.

Articulated locomotives

A distinctive type of locomotive was the articulated. These locomotives featured two sets of drivers under a single boiler—making them basically two engines in one. Each engine/driver set had two cylinders (one on each side), for a total of four on the locomotive.

Early articulateds were actually fairly small, used often on logging lines or other railroads with tight curves and steep grades. By the early 1900s, large articulated locomotives had found a niche in heavy freight service, especially in mountainous territory.

An early type of articulated, first appearing in 1904, was the "Mallet," named after its designer, Anatole Mallet. The Mallet was a compound locomotive, where steam from two cylinders—instead of being released out the exhaust stack—was reused in the other two cylinders, conserving steam. The design was successful, and Mallets grew in size, becoming powerful (but slow) locomotives.

Mallets' lack of speed became a limitation, and from the 1920s onward, larger boilers with higher operating pressure eliminated the need for compounding. Modern articulateds were fast as well as powerful, culminating in designs such as the 4-6-6-4 Challenger and 4-8-8-4 Big Boy.

Geared locomotives

Geared locomotives were designed for industrial and logging lines, where the pounding action of side rods would damage light (or poorly laid) track. Geared locomotives lacked standard drivers—instead, cylinders powered a driveshaft geared to two or three trucks.

The most common was the Shay, with about 2,700 built from 1880 to 1945. The Shay used vertical cylinders on one side to turn a longitudinal driveshaft. The driveshaft then powered wheels on two or three trucks.

Next most common was the Climax (1,100 produced). The Climax had an inclined (angled) cylinder on each side that turned a transverse driveshaft; that driveshaft was geared to a central longitudinal driveshaft under the boiler that provided power to the trucks.

The Heisler was the third most common, with about 600 built. The Heisler used a cylinder on each side, each pointing downward under the boiler (in a V), to drive a longitudinal drive shaft. The shaft powered one axle on each truck; side rods carried the motion to the other axle.

Peak and rapid decline

By the 1930s, new, modern steam locomotives were powerful machines. Many exceeded 5,000 horsepower, a higher rating than a single diesel locomotive of today. They could pull mile-long freight trains at 50 or 60 mph, or heavy passenger trains at 90 mph.

However, diesels were beginning to make inroads in the 1930s, first for switching and high-speed lightweight passenger trains. The appearance of mainline freight locomotives in the form of Electro-Motive's FT in 1939 effectively foretold the end of steam.

The newfangled diesels of the 1930s and 1940s were much more expensive than steam locomotives. However, diesels required little more than periodic refueling to keep them going. They didn't have to stop for water (a huge factor in desert and arid areas) and they had to stop less frequently for fuel. Diesels had no ash pans to dump and no boiler flues that required regular cleaning. Maintenance was much easier with diesels, generally using off-the-shelf parts—extensive steam shops were no longer needed.

And, although individual diesels weren't as powerful as steam locomotives, diesels had advantages in that as many as needed could be coupled together under the control of one engineer, and the same diesels that ran on flatlands could take on the mountains.

Some steam locomotives lasted in service into the 1950s, but by 1960 the steam locomotive had vanished from mainline service in North America.

USRA locomotive types

Type	Driver diameter (inches)	Cylinders (inches)	Total weight (pounds)	Weight on drivers (pounds)	Tractive effort (pounds)	Number built
0-6-0	51	21 x 28	163,000	163,000	39,100	255
0-8-0	51	25 x 28	214,000	214,000	51,000	175
2-8-2 (light)	63	26 x 30	292,000	220,000	54,700	625
2-8-2 (heavy)	63	27 x 32	320,000	239,000	60,000	233
2-10-2 (light)	57	27 x 32	352,000	276,000	69,600	94
2-10-2 (heavy)	63	30 x 32	380,000	293,000	73,800	175
2-6-6-2	57	23, 35 x 32	448,000	358,000	80,000	30
2-8-8-2	57	25, 39 x 32	531,000	474,000	101,300C 121,600S	106
4-6-2 (light)	73	25 x 28	277,000	162,000	40,700	81
4-6-2 (heavy)	79	27 x 28	306,000	197,000	43,900	20
4-8-2 (light)	69	27 x 30	327,000	224,000	53,900	47
4-8-2 (heavy)	69	28 x 30	352,000	243,000	58,200	15

Milwaukee Road no. 360 was one of 233 USRA heavy Mikados (2-8-2s) built. The design was popular, with another 724 copies built following the end of USRA control. *Trains magazine collection*

Notable exceptions to the customized nature of steam locomotives were those designed and built under the direction of the United States Railroad Administration (USRA). The USRA was formed in December 1917, when President Woodrow Wilson placed all of the country's railroads under government control. Railroads were struggling with the demands of World War I traffic, and Wilson nationalized the railroads to improve service and efficiency.

Railroads were short on locomotives, and part of the USRA's directive was to develop common locomotive designs that could be built by any manufacturer for any railroad. Designs for 12 wheel arrangements and types were developed by teams of engineers from the builders and several railroads, including multiple (light and heavy) versions of four types (see the chart above).

The USRA allocated locomotives to various railroads based on need. The first were delivered in July 1918. More than 1,800 locomotives were built to these designs before control reverted back to individual railroads in March 1920.

Most USRA designs proved to be solid, and in following years individual railroads ordered more than 3,000 locomotives to various USRA designs. Known as USRA copies or clones, the most common was the 0-8-0 switcher; even though only 175 were built under USRA control, another 1,200 copies were eventually produced.

1

CHAPTER THREE

Steam locomotive models

In 2007, Athearn added a Union Pacific 4-8-4 to its Genesis series (above). The supurb model features many factory- and modeler-installed details and included a Digital Command Control (DCC) dual-mode sound decoder.

Today is by far the best time in our hobby's history to model the steam era, **1**. For many years, the only way to get railroad-specific steam locomotives was to buy limited-run brass models. Though brass models were well detailed, they came at a premium price and often came up short in terms of performance.

2

This Associated Hobby Manufacturers (AHM) Union Pacific class FEF 4-8-4 steam locomotive was produced in the early 1980s. The direct-current model featured a plastic body, molded and separately applied details, and scale 80" drivers.

Today's HO and N scale steam locomotive models rival brass in level of detail and often surpass them in performance. There's also a wider range of models commercially available. As Chapter 2 mentioned, steam locomotives were largely custom-built for specific railroads and even more specifically for certain regions or uses. This has made it challenging for model manufacturers, as—other than USRA (United States Railroad Administration) designs, they can't simply make a generic 4-6-2 and have it be realistic for more than one or two railroads.

In addition to longtime favorites like the Union Pacific 4-8-8-4 Big Boy and 2-6-0 Moguls, manufacturers are offering railroad-specific models never before released in plastic, such as a Pennsylvania RR class M1a 4-8-2 and Milwaukee Road streamlined class A 4-4-2 (famous for that railroad's *Hiawatha* passenger trains).

Let's take a look at how to get the most out of steam locomotive models. We'll look at basic model construction, weathering and detailing, and maintenance to keep your models running for years to come.

Among today's steam locomotive model manufacturers are Athearn (HO and N), Atlas (N), Bachmann (HO and N), Broadway Limited Imports (HO and N), Con-Cor (N), Fox Valley Models (HO and N), InterMountain Railway Co. (HO and N), International Hobby Corp. (HO), Kato (N), Mantua (HO), Model Power (HO and N), MTH Electric Trains (HO),

3

Bachmann's N scale United States Railroad Administration 2-6-6-2 steam locomotive uses a one-piece plastic boiler and cab seated atop a die-cast metal chassis. Most of the boiler area is filled with a weight. The portion of weight above the firebox can be removed to add a Digital Command Control decoder. *Jim Forbes*

4

Bachmann's HO scale USRA heavy 4-8-2 Mountain has a die-cast metal boiler with many separately applied parts. *Jim Forbes*

5

Sunset Models' HO scale Northern Pacific class Z-8 4-6-6-4 articulated is an example of a contemporary brass steam engine. The model includes a dual-mode QSI Titan stereo sound decoder. *Bill Zuback*

6

This HO New York, New Haven & Hartford class I-5 4-6-4 steam locomotive is part of the Broadway Limited Imports Brass Hybrid line. The locomotive and tender each have a brass body; both feature a die-cast metal chassis.

7

The tender on Bachmann's N scale 2-10-2 Santa Fe is injection-molded plastic. Features include a coal load; separately applied grab irons, uncoupling lever, and ladder; and a "doghouse" behind the coal bunker for the head brakeman. *Jim Forbes*

8

Under the tender shell of Bachmann's N scale 2-8-4 is a printed-circuit board and downward-facing speaker enclosed in the tender floor. *Bill Zuback*

Rivarossi (HO), Sunset Models (HO), Trix (HO), and Wm. K. Walthers (HO and N).

Steam locomotives have evolved tremendously over the years. Take for example the HO scale Union Pacific class FEF (Four Eight Four) 4-8-4 Northern steam locomotive. In 1981, Associated Hobby Manufacturers, better known as AHM, produced its UP 4-8-4. The model, **2**, featured a plastic shell, molded and separately applied details, a non-functioning Mars light, and electrical pickup only from the locomotive. Though the paint was smooth, the yellow stripes and lettering weren't completely opaque.

Fast forward to 2007 when Athearn released its UP 4-8-4, **1**. The high-end Genesis series model has separately applied piping and handrails, a detailed backhead, a working Mars light, and a brass bell. The Athearn 4-8-4 also includes modeler-installed details, such as a wood tender deck, an open pilot, and an operating front knuckle coupler.

Athearn's model also features a dual-mode Digital Command Control (DCC) sound decoder, two speakers in the tender, a die-cast metal frame, a motor with two brass flywheels, rear drivers with traction tires, and chemically blackened cranks and rods. The locomotive is connected to the decoder in the tender via a six-wire plug.

In a review of the AHM 4-8-4 published in the March 1981 *Model Railroader*, it was noted that "The biggest performance handicap is the motor, which has a severe cogging action that limits its low speed." The starting speed was 10.23 scale mph at 2V. The top speed of 74 scale mph, less than that of the prototype, was achieved at 12V. The model could pull 85 freight cars on straight and level track.

When operated on direct current, the Athearn model started moving at a scale 5 mph at 7V (sound-equipped engines have a higher starting voltage on DC). The 4-8-4 achieved a top speed of a scale 95 mph, close to that of the full-size engine. The model had a similar speed range using 128 speed steps in DCC. It can pull 137 freight cars on straight and level track.

Model construction

The way steam locomotives are assembled varies among manufacturers. A construction method favored by several manufacturers is to put an injection-molded plastic boiler and cab (either a single piece or two separate castings) on top of a die-cast metal chassis, **3**. Some manufacturers will add a weight inside the portion of the boiler not occupied by the motor to give the model additional pulling power.

A variation of this design is to use die-cast metal instead of plastic for the cab and/or boiler, **4**. Once the model is painted and the separate plastic and metal details have been added, it's usually impossible to distinguish a die-cast metal model from plastic.

Some of you may be wondering what happened to brass. Though not as common as they once were, brass steam engines are still in production, **5**. These models combine the details brass has long been known for with today's technology, such as dual-mode sound decoders. Since the models are produced in limited numbers, they come with a higher price tag, usually two or three times that of a plastic or die-cast metal model.

In addition to traditional brass models, Broadway Limited Imports (BLI) developed the Brass Hybrid line, **6**. Models in this line have a brass locomotive and tender body with a die-cast metal chassis under each. Other features are typical of those found on traditional BLI steam locomotives, such as a dual-mode sound decoder, a synchronized smoke unit, and painted crew figures.

Steam locomotive tenders can be made of plastic, die-cast metal, or brass, **7**, often following the construction of the locomotive. Inside the body of most tenders is the electronic system and, if sound equipped, one or more speakers, **8**. Some manufacturers also conceal control switches under the hatch covers or other detail parts, **9**.

On some smaller steam locomotives, where there's limited room in the small boiler, the motor may be housed in the tender, **10**. In these situations, the motor is usually linked to the drivers via a drive shaft, **11**.

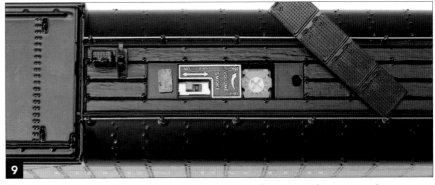

The on/off switch for the smoke unit and the sound system volume control are located under the tender's water hatches on this MTH Electric Trains HO scale Southern Pacific class GS-4 4-8-4. *Jim Forbes*

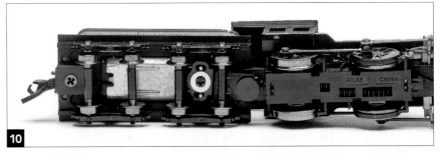

Atlas' N scale 4-4-0 American has the motor mounted in the tender. *Jim Forbes*

The motor in the tender is connected to the drivers with a plastic ball-and-socket driveshaft. *Jim Forbes*

Electrical pickup varies among steam locomotive models. This Bachmann N scale 2-8-4 picks up electrical current through its drivers and tender wheels. *Jim Forbes*

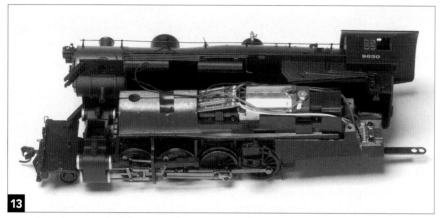

13 This photo shows the drawbar on Bachmann's HO scale United States Railroad Administration 2-8-2 light Mikado. The outer hole allows the locomotive and tender to negotiate tight-radius curves. The inner hole allows for closer coupling. *Bill Zuback*

14 A six-pin plug under the locomotive bridge plate (left) matches the six-pin socket in the tender (right) of BLI's HO scale 4-6-4 Hudson. Note the cab detail. *Jim Forbes*

15 On the new MTH Electric Trains HO scale Pennsylvania RR class H10s, a wireless two-pin connection electrically links the locomotive and tender. *Bill Zuback*

Electrical pickup and tender connections

Another variable of model steam locomotives is electrical pickup. The electrical pickup in the Bachmann N scale 2-8-4, **12**, is through the eight drivers and the six wheels of the rear tender truck. In some instances, if a driver isn't used for electrical pickup, it's fitted with a rubber traction tire to improve the model's pulling ability.

Connecting the tender to the locomotive is often a two-part process. The first is the physical connection between the locomotive and tender via the drawbar. Many manufacturers have drawbars with two holes, **13**. The inner-most hole allows for close coupling between the locomotive and tender, which is best suited for layouts with large-radius curves. The hole closer to the tender allows steam locomotives to negotiate tighter curves. The trade-off is a bigger (less-realistic) gap between the locomotive and tender.

The second connection between the tender and locomotive is electrical. Most locomotives use a wired pin plug that connects with a corresponding socket in the locomotive, **14**. These wires attached to the plug are sometimes difficult to conceal and can be unsightly. On newer models, the drawbar and electrical connection is often combined into one wireless connection, **15**.

Be aware that models with dual-mode DCC decoders often have a higher starting voltage on standard direct-current layouts. The full complement of sound functions on dual-mode models is also limited when operating on DC. Some companies, like Broadway Limited Imports, include configuration variables (CVs) to adjust DC performance. Broadway Limited also sells the DC Master analog control module to control the whistle and additional sound effects.

Painting and weathering tips

Sometimes steam locomotives aren't available in the paint scheme you may want, but that's not a problem. In many cases, a factory-painted model can be repainted and decaled without having to completely disassemble the

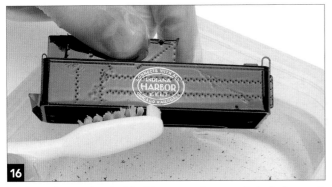

16 Soaking the tender shell in 91 percent isopropyl alcohol was all that was necessary to remove the paint and lettering from the Life-Like Proto 2000 tender shell. *Bill Zuback*

17 New road number decals, applied over a clear gloss finish, helped transform this former Indiana Harbor Belt model into a Virginian Ry. workhorse. *Jim Forbes*

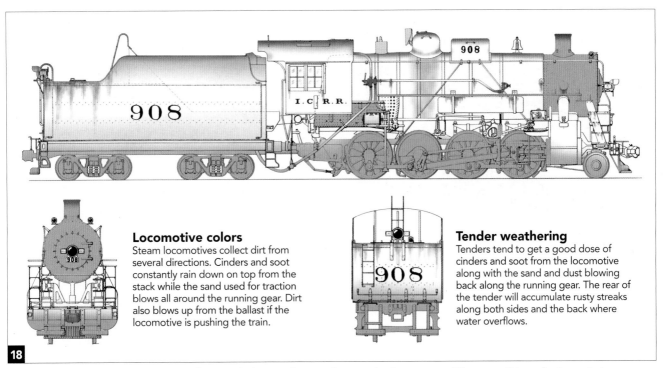

Locomotive colors
Steam locomotives collect dirt from several directions. Cinders and soot constantly rain down on top from the stack while the sand used for traction blows all around the running gear. Dirt also blows up from the ballast if the locomotive is pushing the train.

Tender weathering
Tenders tend to get a good dose of cinders and soot from the locomotive along with the sand and dust blowing back along the running gear. The rear of the tender will accumulate rusty streaks along both sides and the back where water overflows.

18 This illustration provides suggestions for a typical steam locomotive weathering pattern. When possible, refer to prototype photos when weathering a model. *Rick Johnson*

model. A few years ago I was given a Life-Like Proto 2000 (now Wm. K. Walthers) 0-8-0 decorated for the Indiana Harbor Belt. My task was to re-letter and weather the model for the Virginian Ry.

To do this, I first removed the tender shell and soaked it in 91 percent isopropyl alcohol. This caused the factory-applied paint and lettering to lift off the shell, **16**.

Re-lettering the cab was equally easy. I removed the lettering with a cotton swab soaked in Pine-Sol. After cleaning the area to remove any impurities, I sprayed the area under the cab with Microscale Micro Gloss.

After that dried, I added numbers from a Virginian Ry. steam locomotive decal set from Microscale, **17**.

Painting and decaling are fairly straightforward on plastic and die-cast metal steam locomotives. However, many modelers are reluctant to weather their models out of fear of ruining them. With a bit of patience and practice, you can add basic weathering to any model. The illustrations in **18** provide some suggestions for weathering steam locomotives.

You can get your feet wet weathering a steam locomotive using powdered pastel chalks. *Model Railroader* contributing editor Tony Koester used

PanPastels (panpastel.com) applied with a sponge to weather an HO scale Nickel Plate Road Berkshire in 7 minutes, **19**. An advantage with pastels and chalks is that they're very forgiving: You can simply wipe off any effect that doesn't turn out well.

Airbrush weathering may not be for beginners, but it can also yield realistic results. Just use caution when weathering the drivers, rods, and valve gear. To prevent paint from gumming up these parts, apply thinned paint while the locomotive is in motion, **20**. Clean any acrylic paint that gets on the treads of the drivers with a cotton swab dipped in Windex.

19

Ten colors of PanPastel weathering powders and a sponge were all Tony Koester needed to weather this HO steam locomotive—and he did it in just 7 minutes. *Tony Koester*

20

To ensure even coverage of the weathering colors and prevent the working parts from gumming up, I weathered the rods, drivers, and valve gear on this 0-8-0 while the model was under power. *Jim Forbes*

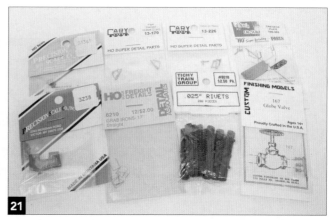

21

A tremendous variety of detail parts for HO scale steam locomotives are available from several manufacturers including Cal-Scale, Cary, Custom Finishing, Detail Associates, Precision Scale, and Tichy.

22

Converting a stock Mantua 0-8-0 to a Central of New Jersey prototype required a lot of work. Alan Mende added more than two dozen detail castings to the boiler alone. *Alan Mende*

23

The late John Pryke revised details and added new plumbing to a budget-priced International Hobby Corp. HO scale 2-6-0 Mogul. *John Pryke*

Detail upgrades

Enhancing a steam locomotive can be done easily with detail parts. Among the manufacturers are Bowser (HO), Cal-Scale (HO), Cary Locomotive Co. (HO), Custom Finishing Models (HO), Detail Associates (HO and N), Gold Medal Models (N), Greenway Products (HO), Miniatures by Eric (HO and N), Precision Scale Co. (HO and N), Selley Finishing Touches (HO), and Tichy Train Group (HO), **21**.

So what can you do with all these detail parts? Quite a bit. Alan Mende modified a Mantua 0-8-0 to more closely match a Central of New Jersey prototype. After removing unwanted molded plastic parts, he added more than two dozen metal castings to the boiler alone, **22**.

A full-fledged re-detailing isn't always necessary. Sometimes replacing molded details with separately applied metal parts can greatly improve the appearance of a budget-priced model, **23**. Detail upgrades can also make today's well-appointed models look even better, **24**.

Space precludes step-by-step directions for all detail parts and situations, as techniques vary by part and model. However, the methods of adding details are similar. Start small—

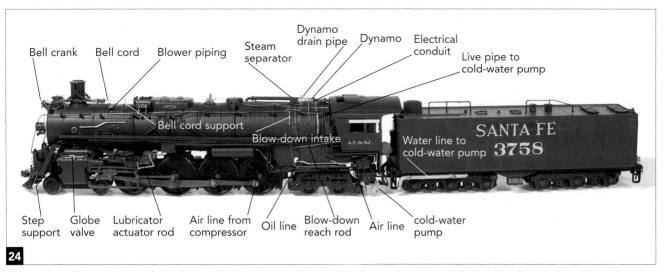

Bell crank   Bell cord   Blower piping   Steam separator   Dynamo drain pipe   Dynamo   Electrical conduit   Live pipe to cold-water pump

Bell cord support

Blow-down intake

Water line to cold-water pump   SANTA FE 3758

Step support   Globe valve   Lubricator actuator rod   Air line from compressor   Oil line   Blow-down reach rod   Air line   cold-water pump

24

Gil Bennet added a variety of details to Ted York's HO scale Broadway Limited Imports Atchison, Topeka & Santa Fe 3751-class 4-8-4. *Ted York*

perhaps a new headlight, compressor, or dome—and you'll gain confidence to do additional detailing. The process often starts with scraping off a model's original detail with a hobby knife, then carefully sanding the surface smooth (generally starting with 200-grit paper, then moving to 400- and 600-grit for a smooth surface).

New plastic, brass, or white-metal details can be glued in place with cyanoacrylate adhesive (CA, or super glue). Some parts have mounting pegs that require matching mounting holes be drilled; wire pieces (handrails, grab irons, and piping) should have mounting holes that they slip into. Always take your time to make sure each detail fits properly in its place, with no unrealistic gaps.

No matter what type of model you start with, always refer to prototype photos when adding details. In the steam era, the type of parts used and their placement often varied between engines within a single class on a railroad. Books on specific railroads (or locomotives) are a great source of information, as are railroad historical society webpages. Also, many modelers have shared ideas, techniques, and tips online when detailing specific models of prototype locomotives.

DCC and steam

Steam locomotives have always had a "cool" factor because of the exposed moving parts: Seeing the rods and

25

Athearn's upgraded Model Die Casting HO scale 2-8-0 has a printed-circuit (PC) board in the tender with a plug for a Digital Command Control decoder. There's also room below the PC board for adding a speaker. *Jim Forbes*

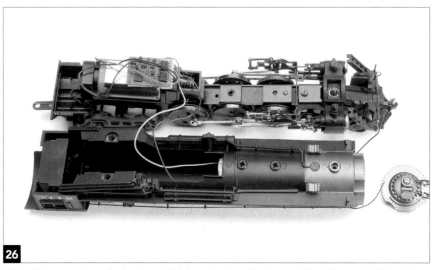

26

Mike Polsgrove installed a Lenz Gold-series decoder in an older Rivarossi HO scale 4-6-4 Hudson. He initially thought about installing the decoder in the tender, but found plenty of room inside the boiler. *Jim Forbes*

Whistle signals

(From *The Standard Code of Operating Rules,* adopted March 1949)

Rule 14. ENGINE WHISTLE SIGNALS

NOTE: The signals prescribed are illustrated by "o" for short sounds; "–" for longer sounds; and "– – –" for extra long sounds. The sounds of the whistle should be distinct, with intensity and duration proportionate to the distance the signal is to be conveyed.

Sound	Indication
(a) o	Apply brakes. Stop.
(b) – –	Release brakes. Proceed.
(c) – o o o	Flagman protect rear of train.
(d) – – – –	Flagman may return from west or south.
(e) – – – – –	Flagman may return from east or north.
(g) o o	Answer to any signal not otherwise provided for.
(h) o o o	When train is standing, back. Answer to 12(d) and 16(c) [trainmen's signals to back]. When train is running, answer to 16(d) [signal to stop at next station].
(j) o o o o	Call for signals.
(k) – o o	(Single track.) To call attention of engine and train crews of trains of the same class, inferior trains, and yard engines, and of trains at train order meeting and waiting points, to signals displayed for a following section. If not answered by a train, the train displaying signals must stop and ascertain the cause unless otherwise provided. (Two or more tracks.) To call attention of engine and train crews, and yard engines, to signals displayed for a following section.
(l) – – o –	Approaching public crossings at grade. To be prolonged or repeated until crossing is reached.
(m) – – – – – – –	Approaching stations, junctions, railroad crossings at grade, and other locations as may be required.
(n) – – o	Approaching meeting or waiting points (see Rule S-90).
(o) o –	Inspect train line for leak or for brakes sticking.
(p) Succession of short sounds.	Alarm for persons or livestock on the track.
(q) – o	Where there are two main tracks on which movements are made in either direction by signal indications, trains on left track will sound this signal preceding signal 14(d) or 14(e). When running against the current of traffic: (1) Approaching stations, curves, or other points where view may be obscured. (2) Approaching passenger or freight trains and when passing freight trains. (3) Preceding the signals prescribed by (d), (e), and others as prescribed by rule.

valve gear in motion as the locomotive rolls along is certainly appealing. This has been further enhanced with Digital Command Control (DCC), especially with sound features such as chuff, bell, whistle, and air compressors. Other DCC advantages include the ability to have realistic speed ranges and lighting features. Manufacturers often include basic DCC programming information in the model's instruction booklet and on their websites.

Most of today's models are offered with a DCC decoder (often with sound) already installed, or have provisions for adding one, **25**. If you have an older model without provisions for a decoder, don't worry. In most cases, you should be able to add a decoder speaker, **26**. The details of this are beyond the scope of this book, but there are many publications (such as *DCC Projects and Applications*, Volumes 2 and 3), that will help walk you through the process.

Keeping steam running

Today's steam locomotive models are nearly maintenance free. However, there are times when repairs might be necessary. Photos **27** and **28** show the main external detail and drive train components of a steam locomotive.

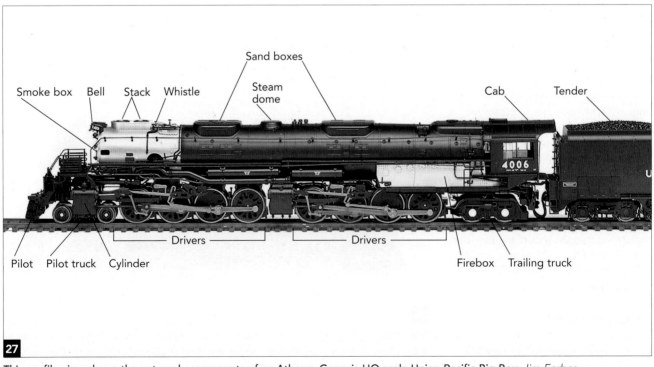

27

This profile view shows the external components of an Athearn Genesis HO scale Union Pacific Big Boy. *Jim Forbes*

On today's models, the motor is usually located in the boiler or cab, **29**. The motor typically powers one pair of drivers using a worm and worm gear, **30**. Cast-metal side rods transfer motion to the other drivers.

The motor on most locomotives can be reached by removing a screw or screws under the frame, **30**. If you have difficulty finding the screw, check for an exploded-view diagram of the model in the instructions. The tender is usually secured by two or more screws. Most are located on the bottom of the chassis, **31**. Sometimes the screws are in less obvious locations, such as under the coal bunker. Tender shells on N scale steam locomotives may be press-fit or secured with tabs.

About the only maintenance required on steam locomotives is periodic lubrication, **32**. Most models are lubricated at the factory prior to shipment, and many of the plastics used on today's models are self-lubricating. Therefore, you should be able to run your steam locomotive for quite a while before any lubrication is necessary.

Key points to lubricate with light oil are the driver bearings, armature bearings on the motor, worm gear shaft bearings, and side rods at the crank pins. Use light grease on the gears.

Make sure all lubricants are plastic compatible. Remember, a drop or two of lubricant is all that's necessary. Applying too much oil or grease can be just as damaging as not adding enough. If you're not sure what parts should be lubricated, refer to the instruction sheet included with the model.

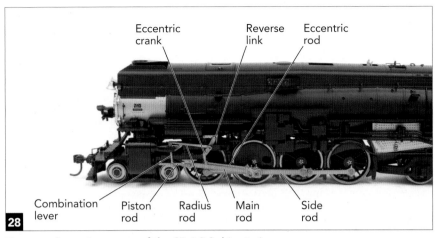

28 Here are the various parts of the SP 4-8-2 drive train.

29 A single screw under the frame is all that holds the boiler and cab to the chassis on this Trix HO scale 2-8-2 Mikado. *Jim Forbes*

30 A can motor with a single flywheel is concealed in the boiler of Broadway Limited's HO scale K4s. A worm and worm gear power the middle drivers; cast-metal side rods transfer power to the other drivers. *Jim Forbes*

31 Screws that hold the tender body in place are often located along the edges of the chassis.

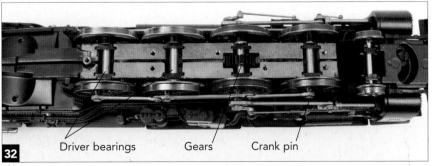

32 Periodic lubrication is usually all that's necessary to keep modern steam locomotive models running smoothly. The driver bearings and gears should be lubricated with light oil and light grease, respectively.

1

CHAPTER FOUR

Prototype diesel locomotives

Electro-Motive Division's best-selling locomotive model was the SD40-2. Dakota, Minnesota & Eastern no. 6363 is one of more than 3,900 of the six-axle road units built between 1972 and 1986. The 3,000-hp locomotive proved versatile, finding its niche on railroads across the country in fast-freight and drag-freight service.

Diesel locomotives have been used on railroads since the 1930s, with dieselization progressing quickly in the 1940s and into the '50s. By the late 1950s, steam locomotives on Class 1 railroads were pretty much gone. Locomotive builders have come and gone since the diesel era began, and the appearance of diesels has evolved. There have been some duds along the way, but there have been some major successes, such as the EMD SD40-2, **1**, the best-selling model in EMD's history.

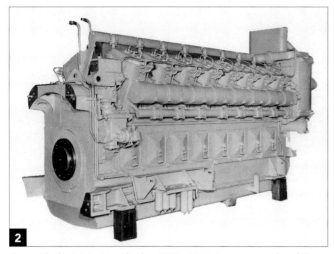

General Electric's 16-cylinder 7FDL-16A1 is an example of the large engines used in road diesel locomotives.
Trains magazine collection

The Electro-Motive FT was the first successful road freight diesel. At 1,350 hp each, this A-B-B-A set of FTs combined for 5,400 hp. *R.H. Payne; Louis A. Marre collection*

Norfolk Southern no. 2655, a current-production EMD SD70M-2, is typical of modern road-freight diesels. Rated at 4,300 hp, this single six-axle locomotive has more horsepower than three FTs.

The wheels on diesel locomotives are powered by electric traction motors mounted on each axle. This D-57 traction motor was introduced by EMD in October 1961. *EMD*

In this chapter, we'll look at how prototype diesels work, identify internal and external components, and take a look at some of the switchers, freight locomotives, and passenger diesels used by railroads over the past 75-plus years.

How diesel locomotives work

Diesel locomotives are powered by, as you probably guessed, a diesel engine, **2**. The size and style of engine has changed over the years, and varies between manufacturers. For example, Electro-Motive's pioneering FT of 1939 had a 16-cylinder 567 or 567A diesel engine rated at 1,350 hp, **3**. Today's Electro-Motive SD70M-2 has a 16-cylinder 16-710G3C-T2 diesel

engine rated at 4,300 hp, **4**.

The diesel engine doesn't drive the wheels directly. Instead, it drives an electric generator or alternator. The electricity is then regulated and used to power an electric motor ("traction motor") mounted on each axle, **5**.

Most of a diesel locomotive's mechanical equipment is obscured by a metal hood. Early diesels, such as Electro-Motive Division E- (passenger) and F-series (freight) locomotives and Alco PA (passenger) and FA (freight) locomotives, had full-width carbodies, **6**. Known as "cab units," their design made it difficult to gain access to the engine and other internal components. They were

available with cabs (A units) or as cabless boosters (B units).

Electro-Motive Division general-purpose (GP) road switchers ("Geeps") and Alco RS-series ("road switchers") had narrower hoods with access doors and walkways, providing easier engine access, **7**. Known as "hood units," this basic design was adopted by manufacturers for most freight locomotives from the early 1950s onward. The photo in **8** shows the other internal components of an EMD SD9 (for EMD, the SD indicated six axles; a GP had four axles).

Locomotive control and braking is done from a control stand or desktop-style console, **9**. The throttle handle is

6

Electro-Motive Division E units, such as Florida East Coast E3 no. 1001, had full-width carbodies. Early Es had long, slanted noses compared to F units and late Es. *William L. Wedemeyer*

7

Independent Locomotive Service GP9 no. 1334, a General Motors Diesel Division (Canada) GP9, illustrates the road switcher body, featuring a narrow hood with side walkways.

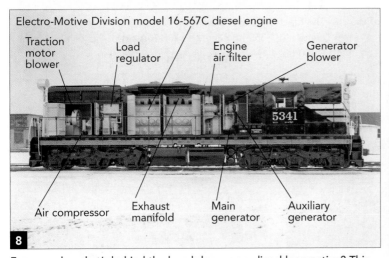

Electro-Motive Division model 16-567C diesel engine

Traction motor blower · Load regulator · Engine air filter · Generator blower

Air compressor · Exhaust manifold · Main generator · Auxiliary generator

8

Ever wonder what's behind the hood doors on a diesel locomotive? This photo reveals the internal components of Southern Pacific SD9 no. 5341. *Trains magazine collection*

Brake pressure gauges

Dynamic brake

Automatic brake

Reverser

Throttle

9

Control features vary among locomotives, but this control stand on an EMD GP40-2 is typical of most diesels. *Ernest L. Novak*

moved from left to right. Most diesels have nine notches (idle and 1 through 8); notching the control up increases engine RPMs, which increases power. If you look closely, you'll see that the throttle handle has its flat surfaces oriented horizontally. That makes it easier to distinguish by feel the throttle handle from that of the dynamic brake, which has the flat surfaces positioned vertically.

The uppermost lever is the dynamic brake, which is moved from left to right. It locks in two positions, off (as shown in the photo) and set up. It moves through the rest of its range, 1 through 8. Dynamic braking turns the traction motors into generators, providing resistance to turning that serves as braking power. Dynamic braking is primarily used for controlling train speeds on descending grades.

The reverser handle is located below

the throttle and has three positions: left, center, and right. When the handle is moved right, the locomotive is set up to move forward. Moving the handle left sets the locomotive up to move in reverse. If the reverser is centered, the dynamic brake handle can't move because of a mechanical interlocking. Though the throttle will still move, power isn't sent to the traction motors.

Two additional brake systems are used. The automatic brake applies and releases the train brakes by removing air from (or adding air to) the train line, the system of pipes and air hoses that run the length of the train. This action triggers control valves on each car to apply or release the brake shoes, which apply pressure on the wheels.

The independent brake, below the automatic brake, operates the locomotive's brakes separate from the train.

What's on the outside?

Unlike steam locomotives, diesel locomotives are fairly standardized with common parts and built in assembly-line fashion, meaning an SW1500 on the Wisconsin Central is going to look fairly similar to one on the BNSF, **10**. To further understand the external parts of a locomotive, look at the Grand Trunk Western GP38-2 in **11**.

Where the variations come into play is on the small details. For example, railroads use headlights in varying styles from multiple manufacturers; some railroads prefer mounting headlights above the cab windows between the number boards, while others like them on the nose. The bell can be under the walkway, on the hood, or on the nose. Air horn styles vary widely from railroad to railroad. Some railroads opt for cab air conditioners or pilot-mounted plows; others do not.

These locomotives are both EMD SW1500 switchers. At first glance, other than paint, the two locomotives look the same. However, look closely and you'll see they have different trucks, air horns, and exhaust stack spark arrestors.

Diesel Details

Firecracker antenna · Sand hatch · Headlights · Number board · Cab · Radiator fans · Air horn · Radiator screen · Short hood · Ditch lights · Coupler · M.U. Cables · Plow · Bell · Fuel filler · Fuel gauge · Fuel tank · Truck

Grand Trunk Western GP38-2 no. 5849 is a fairly typical example of the more than 2,200 of the four-axle road units that were built by Electro-Motive Division between 1972 and 1986.

Types of locomotives

In the 75-plus years of diesel locomotives, there have been a handful of major manufacturers and a wide variety of locomotives. The major manufacturers include General Motors Electro-Motive Division (and General Motors Diesel Division in Canada), General Electric, Alco, Baldwin Locomotive Works, Lima-Hamilton, and Fairbanks-Morse.

The last Baldwin diesel was built in 1956, and the final Fairbanks-Morse locomotive for the domestic market rolled off the assembly line two years later. Alco quit making locomotives in 1969. General Motors sold EMD to a firm called Electro-Motive Diesel in 2005; five years later, Caterpillar-owned Progress Rail Services purchased Electro-Motive Diesel. Today, GE and EMD are the big two of diesel locomotive manufacturing.

Although there are many subcategories and crossovers, diesel locomotives can be broadly categorized into three basic types: switchers, road freight locomotives, and passenger engines. You'll find each builder's locomotives has a distinctive appearance, and with some practice, you'll be better able to identify them by things such as cab style and shape, hood shape, location and style of details (fans, exhaust stacks, number boards, etc.), and type of trucks.

A note on model designations: Most manufacturers used basic letter designations to indicate a series or type, with numbers indicating either horsepower or successive (newer) models. Some used additional numbers to indicate the number of axles and/or powered axles. A full explanation of the many variations, with photos, can be found in *The Model Railroader's Guide to Diesel Locomotives* (Kalmbach, 2009).

Switchers

Switching locomotives were among the first successful diesels, gaining

12

There's no hiding the original owner of Burlington Northern SW1 no. 80. Even though production was suspended for three years during World War II, more than 600 of these end-cab switchers were produced. *George H. Drury*

13

More than 1,500 Alco S-2 switchers were built for customers in North America. Soo Line S-2 no. 2105 works the yard in North Fond du Lac, Wis., in 1951. *Stan H. Mailer*

14

This Baldwin VO1000 features the body style used on the end-cab switcher from 1942 until 1946. Baldwin switchers had tall hoods that stopped just short of the cab roofline.
Chicago, Burlington & Quincy

15

General Electric's 44-tonner was a popular lightweight switcher, built from 1939 through 1956. It has a distinctive appearance, with a tall center cab. It has two small diesel engines, one under each hood. *Chicago, Burlington & Quincy*

popularity in the 1930s. Diesels eliminated the smoke problem of steam switchers operating in urban areas, and they required far less-frequent fueling and maintenance. Most diesel switchers feature a full-height cab at one end, with a hood (some had full-height hoods; most had short hoods for better two-way visibility) with walkways on either side. Switchers tend to be low-horsepower, high tractive-effort locomotives, with the emphasis on moving heavy cuts of cars at slow speeds.

Electro-Motive Division's SW1 was a popular early switcher, **12**. Production of the 600-hp switcher, equipped with a 567 diesel engine, lasted from 1939 to 1949, with more than 600 units built for railroads in the United States and Canada. Some can still be found earning their keep at industries and on tourist railroads.

The 567 diesel engine was the backbone of EMD switchers until 1966, when EMD began production on its 1,000-hp SW1000 and 1,500-hp

SW1500. These locomotives featured, respectively, 8- and 12-cylinder 645E diesel engines. Of the two, the SW1500 proved more successful, **10**, staying in production until 1974, with more than 800 units produced.

The last EMD switchers built were the MP15-series (AC, DC, and T). Production of these 1,500-hp units started in 1974 with the MP15DC and wrapped up in 1987 with the MP15T. Between the three models, about 500 units were built.

Alco was an early player in the switcher market, starting with its 60- and 100-ton boxcabs in the 1920s. Alco found its greatest success with its S-series switchers, **13**. The 660-hp S-1 and 1,000-hp S-2 were in production concurrently from 1940 to 1950. The S-2 proved more popular, with more than 1,500 units built for customers in the U. S., Canada, and Mexico.

Though Baldwin had a variety of switchers, its best-selling model was the VO1000, **14**. Produced from 1939 to 1946, the 1,000 hp switcher had a

VO diesel engine (hence the model designation). It could be found on major railroads throughout the United States, including the Atchison, Topeka & Santa Fe; Chicago, Burlington & Quincy; and Pennsylvania RR.

Lima-Hamilton was a minor player in switchers (and diesels), producing only 136 total switchers before the company folded in the early 1950s. Even though Lima (before its merger with Hamilton) was a major steam manufacturer, it didn't begin producing diesels until other builders had saturated the market. Lima-Hamilton switchers had no model designations. Instead, they were classified by horsepower (750, 800, 1,000, and 1,200).

General Electric, like Alco, started in the switcher market with boxcabs in the late 1920s. The locomotive builder's best seller was the 44-ton center-cab switcher, **15**. The model, rated at 400 hp, used a pair of Caterpillar D17000 diesel engines. More than 350 locomotives were built for railroads and industrial users. The locomotives were

16 Milwaukee Road Fairbanks-Morse H-10-44 shows the high (cab-roof-level) hood needed to clear F-M's tall opposed-piston engine. The roof overhang on the back of the cab was a feature on H-10-44s and early H-12-44s. *Milwaukee Road*

17 Electro-Motive wasn't the first to make the hood unit, but they built the most. Chicago & North Western no. 1534 is an example of a GP7. It was EMD's first successful road switcher. *Stan Mailer*

18 The Geep series came to a close in 1994 with the spartan-cab (non-wide-nose) GP60. These two Southern Pacific locomotives were fresh off the assembly line when photographed in Franklin Park, Ill. *David Fasules*

19 Canadian National SD70M-2 no. 8895 illustrates the modern look of Electro-Motive diesels. The red lights by the number boards are marker lights that are illuminated when the locomotive is used at the rear of a train.

popular in that they skirted just under the 45-ton weight limit at which a fireman was required.

Fairbanks-Morse also had a variety of switchers, but the Beloit, Wis.-based builder had its greatest success with the H-10-44 and H-12-44 switchers, **16**. Production of these two models lasted from 1944 until 1961. The switchers are distinct because of their tall hood, needed to house the company's unique opposed-piston diesel engines.

Road freight diesels

The first successful road-freight diesel was the Electro-Motive FT, **3**, introduced in 1939. Even though each unit produced just 1,350 hp (compared to 5,000 horsepower for a "modern" steam locomotive), multiple units could be connected electrically under the control of a single engineer. The FT effectively doomed steam by this versatility. The other huge factor was maintenance: Diesels required no stops for water (a bane of steam, especially in desert areas), fewer stops for fuel,

and much less-frequent maintenance (no ashpans to dump or boiler flues to clean). Off-the-shelf parts meant major repairs were easier, faster, and cheaper to perform.

Electro-Motive Division F-series cab units (FT through F9) were produced into the 1950s and lasted on some railroads into the 1980s.

Streamlined diesels looked good, but made it tough to access the engine and other internal components for maintenance. Also, cab units weren't ideal for switching moves, with limited rearward visibility. This led to the hood-unit (road switcher) design. For EMD, this was the four-axle GP7 in 1949, **17**, basically a hood-unit version of the company's then-current 1,500-hp cab unit F7. EMD began offering six-axle road switchers with the SD7 in 1952. The GP designation stood for "general purpose," and the SD prefix indicated "special duty."

The GP and SD series increased in horsepower through the years, with the 1,800-hp GP18, 2,000-hp GP20,

2,250-hp GP30, 2,500-hp GP35, and 3,000-hp GP40 by the early 1970s (SDs followed a similar path, topped by the 3,600-hp SD45). From 1972 through the 1980s, EMD offered improved versions of the latest of these in its "Dash 2" line, with the GP38-2 and GP40-2 as the most popular four-axle models and the SD40-2 the king of the six-axle diesels, **1**.

By the 1990s, railroads had transitioned to six-axle diesels for most freight service. EMD's last four-axle road diesels were the GP60-series (GP60, GP60M, and GP60B), produced between 1985 and 1994, **18**. The SD-series continued to develop through the SD50 and SD60, and is produced today under Electro-Motive with the SD70ACe and SD70M-2, **19**.

Alco's RS-1, which debuted in 1941, was a trendsetter for the road-switcher design, **20**. The locomotive had a narrow long hood, an inset cab, and tall short hood. In 1946, Alco released its six-axle cousin, the RSD-1. Alco continued offering road switchers with

20

Alco introduced the road switcher design with its RS-1. A cab bookended by a narrow long hood and short hood were design characteristics other builders used when designing their road switchers. *Don Wood*

21

Alco adopted the Century name for its latest line of four- and six-axle road units, which it introduced in the early 1960s. New York Central no. 2058 is a C-430 (4 axles, 3,000 hp). *Ernest L. Novak*

22

Alco introduced its streamlined freight FA-1 and later FA-2 to rival EMD's F units (cabless versions were designated FBs). These two Great Northern FA-1s are on the point of a freight in July 1965. *K.L. Douglas, Louis A. Marre collection*

23

Baldwin was only in the road unit business for a decade, but it found success with its AS-16 road switcher. Baltimore & Ohio was one of nine railroads that operated the 1,600-hp locomotive. *Louis A. Marre collection*

the RS-2 and RS-3 (RSD for six-axle units), continuing through the RSD-15 and RS-27.

The early 1960s saw Alco introduce its Century line of diesels. They had a "C" prefix with four-digit numbers: the first digit signified axles (4 or 6) and the last two digits horsepower. The locomotives had a revised body style compared to earlier locomotives as shown by the 3,000-hp C-430, **21**.

Alco also offered cab-unit freight diesels: the FA-1 and -2, **22**. They weren't as popular as EMD's F unit line, but they became popular among railfans and modelers because of their styling, as they resemble shortened versions of Alco's PA passenger diesels (more on those in a bit).

Baldwin's time in the road unit market was fairly short lived, lasting from 1946-1956. The best seller of its offerings was the four-axle, 1,600-hp AS-16, **23**. The builder's locomotives had a distinctive appearance, with

the ends of the hoods squared off. Baldwin also produced six-axle road locomotives.

Baldwin's cab unit four-axle freight diesels (the nearly identical DR-4-4-15 and RF-16), although built in small numbers, became well-known among modelers and railfans for their unique "sharknose" appearance, **24**.

Fairbanks-Morse H-series four- and six-axle road units were produced from 1947 to 1958. The H-24-66 (known as the Train Master) was the best-known of its offering, **25**. The 2,400-hp locomotive, introduced in 1953, was at the time the highest-horsepower diesel in production.

The F-M Consolidated Line cab-unit locomotives, or C-Liners, were in production from 1950 to 1954. The best seller was the CFA-16-4, with 65 produced for customers in the United States and Canada.

General Electric was a late entry to the road locomotive market,

bringing out the 2,500-hp U25B (U for Universal, 2,500-hp, B for two-axle trucks) in 1959, **26**, after other minor builders had exited the market. In 1963, it unveiled a six-axle version, the U25C. The U25 diesels were successful, and spawned a horsepower race with EMD that would last through the 1960s. Follow-up U-series models included the U28, U30, U33, and U36 (all in B and C versions), through 1975.

GE followed the U series with the Dash 7 and Dash 8 lines. The last four-axle GE road units were Dash 8-40BWs, built in 1991 for the Atchison, Topeka & Santa Fe. General Electric continued building six-axle freight diesels and is currently the leader in diesel locomotive production in North America. Its current line is the Evolution Series (ES44AC, ES44DC, and ES40DC), **27**. These modern units can be found in heavy-haul, fast freight, and general service across the continent.

24

Baldwin didn't have a large list of diesels to its credit, but its RF-16 (and similar DR-4-4-15) cab freight locomotives had the best nickname, "sharknose." Only 168 A units were built. Delaware & Hudson RF-16 no. 1216 poses for the company photographer on Oct. 21, 1974. *Delaware & Hudson*

25

Fairbanks-Morse H-24-66, dubbed the Train Master, was known for its substantial carbody. At 2,400 hp, the Train Master was the highest-horsepower road switcher on the market when introduced in 1953. Number 6301 was one of five Train Masters rostered by the Southern Railway. *Ken Douglas*

26

General Electric rolled out its U-series of locomotives in 1959 with the U25B. Although a latecomer to the road-switcher market, GE would eventually top EMD in sales. *General Electric*

27

CSX no. 5437 is a General Electric ES40DC. Most modern diesels are available with AC or DC traction motors. The AC versions can handle heavier loads, but are more expensive.

Passenger diesels

Passenger diesels found success prior to road freight diesels, with many new streamliners of the 1930s powered by EMD and Alco passenger units. Passenger trains were relatively light compared to freights, but moved at high speeds on tight schedules. Railroads liked that diesels didn't need frequent fuel and water stops, making it easier to keep these schedules.

Passenger locomotives had unique requirements compared to freight engines. They needed room for steam generators (and a water-supply tank), since passenger cars needed steam for heat. They were geared for high speeds (100 mph and faster on some railroads), meaning they sacrificed low-speed tractive effort. They also had to ride smoothly at high speeds. This led to the use of long-wheelbase six-wheel (three-axle) trucks, with the center axle

an unpowered idler and the outer axles equipped with traction motors.

The long trucks and extended carbodies allowed room for two diesel engines in many passenger diesels (early Alcos and all EMD E units), with each engine supplying power to one truck. Even in those with just one engine, passenger diesels were longer and rated at higher horsepower than their contemporary freight engines.

Electro-Motive Division's E-series cab units were the most popular and the most recognizable passenger units of the pre-Amtrak era, **28**. The dual-engine cab units were often painted to match the trains they pulled. Early E units (E3, E4, E5, E6) had long, slanted noses, while the later—and more common—E7, E8, and E9 versions had the same "bulldog" nose of freight F units. The locomotives were also noticeably longer than F units, and

rode on six-wheel trucks. Horsepower progressed from 1,800 on early Es to 2,000 hp for E3 through E7, 2,250 hp for E8, and 2,400 for the E9.

By the 1960s, passenger service was on the decline. Railroads needing new passenger locomotives generally opted for steam-generator-equipped versions of EMD's regular freight units, with the thought that they could be used in standard freight service if passenger trains were eliminated. EMD indicated this with a "P" in the model designation, including the SDP35, SDP40, GP40P, and GP40P-2, **29**.

The coming of Amtrak saw a new passenger locomotive from EMD, the cowl-bodied (enclosed) SDP40F, a six-axle diesel based on the company's SD45 freight engine. The locomotives did not fare well and were taken out of service by the end of the 1970s. Replacing them were the F40PH

This A-B set of Union Pacific E7s shows off the long, sleek body and six-axle trucks of EMD's passenger locomotives. E units were powered by a pair of diesel engines. *Trains magazine collection*

Compared to a standard SD40, Great Northern SDP40 no. 322 has additional space behind the radiator section which houses the steam generator equipment, identifying this as a passenger-service engine. *Trains magazine collection*

Amtrak switched to a four-axle design with the EMD F40PH, which became a successful passenger locomotive for commuter railroads as well. The locomotives are basically GP40-2s with high-speed gearing. *Ralph L. Phillips*

and F40PH-2, four-axle diesels that would become extremely successful and would dominate both long-haul and commuter passenger trains through the 1990s, **30**.

Electro-Motive Division's last passenger unit of quantity was the F59PHI, **31**. The streamlined locomotive has a Fiberglas nose and is used by several commuter passenger agencies. It was built through 2001.

Although EMD dominated the market, Alco produced a significant number of passenger diesels through the 1950s. First came the twin-engine, six-axle, 2,000-hp DL-series locomotives, produced from 1939 through 1945, **32**. They loosely

resembled EMD's E units, but with a much different cab and nose.

Alco followed the DL with a more successful locomotive, the PA, produced from 1946 through 1953, **33**. Although still a six-axle locomotive, the PA used a single engine (2,000 hp for the PA-1; 2,250 for the PA-2). Although a comparatively small number were built, the PAs have become popular among railfans and modelers alike for their distinctive long, wide noses and unique appearance.

General Electric was a latecomer to the passenger game, entering in the 1960s with the U28CG and U30CG, both special orders for a single customer, Santa Fe. The locomotive

builder hit its stride in the passenger business in the mid-1990s with the P42DC, **34**. This unit is operated by Amtrak (which used it to replace EMD F40PHs) and VIA Rail Canada.

It should also be noted that many builders offered their standard freight locomotives with steam generators added for passenger service. Common examples included EMD F units, GP7s, and GP9s. These were often used on secondary and branchline trains where high speed wasn't required. Many railroads preferred F units for passenger service, especially in mountainous territory: Santa Fe, Great Northern, and Northern Pacific were examples.

31

Amtrak California's F59PHI, introduced in the mid-1990s, has a streamlined carbody and side skirts that blend in with the passenger cars that it pulls.
David Lustig

32

The New York, New Haven & Hartford had the largest fleet of Alco DL-109 diesel locomotives (60). The railroad operated the World War II-era units in freight and passenger service.
New York, New Haven & Hartford

33

Nickel Plate Road no. 102 is an example of the PA, Alco's sleek, long-nosed, six-axle postwar passenger diesel. *Paul W. Prescott*

34

General Electric's P42DC can be found leading passenger trains across the United States and Canada. Here, Amtrak nos. 164 and 93 bring the westbound *Empire Builder* through Resseville, Wis.

1

CHAPTER FIVE

Diesel model basics and maintenance

The WalthersTrainline HO scale GP9M is a typical basic-level ready-to-run diesel locomotive model. It has molded grab irons on the rear of the long hood, molded grills and screens, plastic handrails, and printed number boards.

Today's modelers are blessed with an abundance of diesel locomotives in HO and N scales. These models are well-proportioned and feature accurate paint schemes and lettering. Some are even detailed to match a specific road number. In this chapter, we'll look at the different types of locomotives offered in HO and N scales, examine the mechanical differences between the two scales, offer tips on how to upgrade models, explore the types of Digital Command Control decoders available, and show you how to keep your locomotive running well.

2

Bachmann's HO scale GP9 lacks drill-starter points, grab irons, and m.u. cables. Modelers who want to add those details will need to refer to prototype photos. *Jim Forbes*

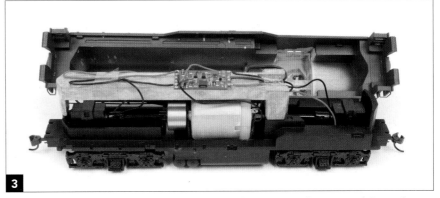

3

Even many basic-level diesel locomotives now feature Digital Command Control motor-only decoders. This is the WalthersTrainline HO scale GP9M.

Wire grab irons

Drill-starter points for eye bolts

4

Most HO and N scale diesel locomotive models fall into the mid-level category. This Athearn Ready-to-Roll HO scale GP40-2 has factory-installed and painted grab irons, drill-starter points for eye bolts on the roof, and molded nubs on the pilots for positioning uncoupling levers and m.u. cables.

Types of models

As with freight cars, there are different levels of diesel locomotive models. Basic ready-to-run models include Athearn (HO scale Roundhouse line), Bachmann (HO and N), Model Power (HO and N), and WalthersTrainline (HO). Basic ready-to-run locomotives, **1**, feature molded-in-place (instead of separate) details and basic painting and lettering. Some, like the Bachmann GP9 in **2**, lack separate or molded grab irons on the hood ends or multiple-unit (m.u.) hoses on the pilots. Without bolt-head detail or drill-starter points (small dimples

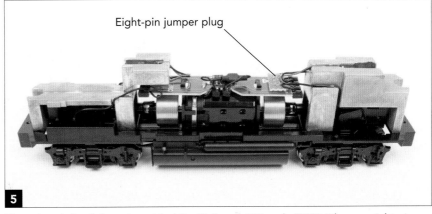

Eight-pin jumper plug

5

The printed-circuit board on this Atlas Trainman HO scale GP38-2 has an eight-pin jumper plug. The model can be converted to Digital Command Control by removing the jumper plug and adding a drop-in decoder with an eight-pin plug.

6

Fox Valley Models is fairly new to the HO scale market, but its models are at the top of the class. Factory-installed and painted grab irons, see-through fan screens, and a detailed cab interior are just some of the highlights of this model.

molded in place), it's up to the modeler to add these, using prototype photos as a guide.

Historically, basic models were only designed to run on standard DC layouts. However, Bachmann, Model Power, and Walthers now offer these models with motor-only decoders for Digital Command Control (DCC) operation, **3**.

Mid-level ready-to-run diesels make up the bulk of the market. Examples include the Athearn Ready-to-Roll line (HO), AthearnN, Atlas Trainman (HO and N), Bachmann

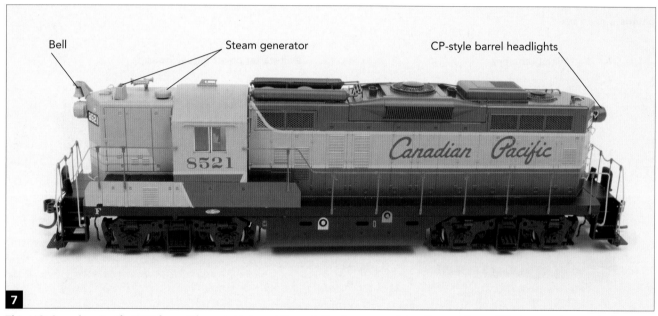

Bell   Steam generator   CP-style barrel headlights

7

This HO Canadian Pacific GP9 from Athearn's high-end Genesis line has several details specific to CP's locomotives, including a nose-mounted bell, steam generator detail on the short hood, winterization hatch, roof-mounted air tanks, and barrel headlights.

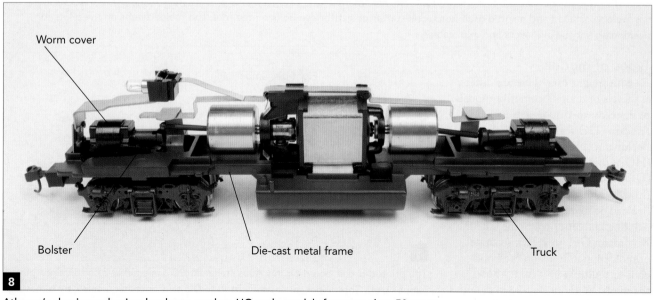

Worm cover

Bolster   Die-cast metal frame   Truck

8

Athearn's classic mechanism has been used on HO scale models for more than 50 years.

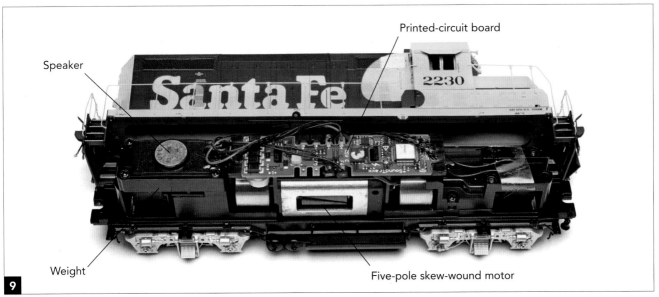

Speaker

Printed-circuit board

2230

Weight

Five-pole skew-wound motor

9

The mechanisms on today's HO scale models are usually covered by a weight or group of weights. The wiring for the model is run through a printed-circuit board that snaps to the top of the weight. This sound-equipped Athearn Genesis model has a speaker over the rear truck. *Jim Forbes*

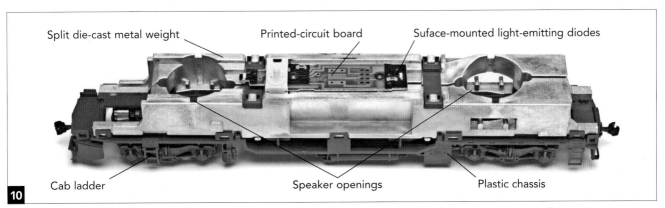

Split die-cast metal weight

Printed-circuit board

Suface-mounted light-emitting diodes

Cab ladder

Speaker openings

Plastic chassis

10

Wait a minute, where's the motor? Instead of using a traditional motor in the middle of the chassis, Kato's HO scale General Electric P42 diesel locomotive has a motor in each truck. *Jim Forbes*

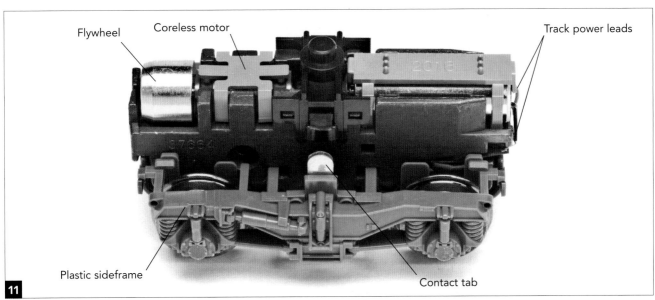

Flywheel

Coreless motor

Track power leads

Plastic sideframe

Contact tab

11

This close-up view shows the motor and flywheel fit in the Kato truck. The trucks are press-fit to the chassis and can easily be removed for maintenance without removing the shell. *Jim Forbes*

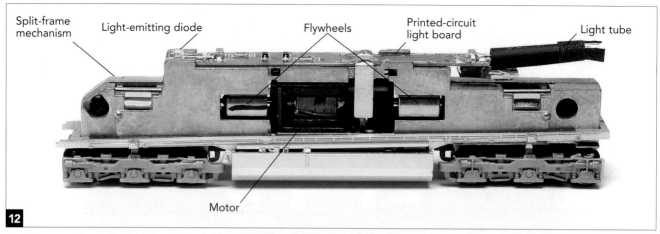

Split-frame mechanism · Light-emitting diode · Flywheels · Printed-circuit light board · Light tube · Motor

12

Here's a typical N scale split-frame mechanism, illustrated by the Fox Valley Models General Electric ES44AC. *Bill Zuback*

Split-frame mechanism · Printed-circuit board · DCC decoder · Speaker

13

There's not much room left under the shell on Athearn's N scale F59PHI diesel locomotive when a Digital Command Control decoder and speaker are added. *Jim Forbes*

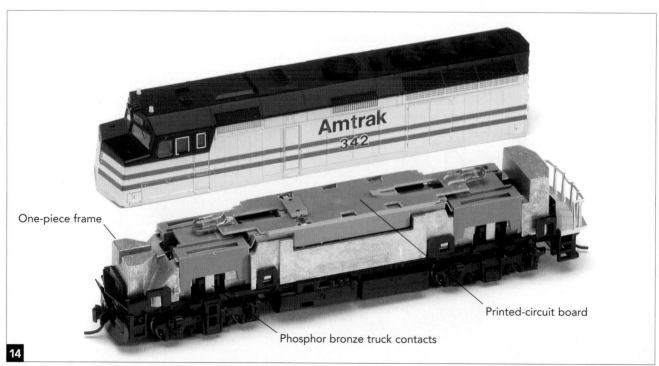

One-piece frame · Printed-circuit board · Phosphor bronze truck contacts

14

Kato took a new approach with the one-piece mechanism on its N scale Electro-Motive Division F40PH diesel locomotive. Instead of using the frame as an electrical path, phosphor bronze truck contacts carry power to the PC board. *Jim Forbes*

Sound Value line (HO and N), Bowser (Stewart Hobbies) Traditional line (HO), WalthersMainline (HO), and WalthersN, **4**. Typical features of these models include some separately applied details or provisions for adding them, multiple road numbers, and the same or similar motor found on the manufacturer's high-end models.

Most companies offer mid-level models in DC and DCC and versions with or without sound. The DC versions often have provisions for a drop-in decoder on the printed-circuit board, and in some cases a dedicated space for adding a speaker, **5**.

A recent trend has been for manufacturers to offer DCC-equipped mid-level models with basic sound decoders. Athearn (HO), Bachmann (HO and N), and Walthers (HO) are examples of companies that produce locomotives with basic SoundTraxx sound decoders. Sound effects may include a long and short air horn or whistle blast, a bell, and diesel engine sounds. The lighting effects are limited, and motor control features are basic.

High-end ready-to-run models include Athearn Genesis (HO), Atlas Master (HO and N), Bachmann Spectrum (HO and N), Broadway Limited Imports (HO and N), Bowser Executive line (HO), Fox Valley Models (HO and N), Hornby Hobbies (Rivarossi in HO, Arnold in N), Kato (HO and N), Rapido Trains (HO and N), and WalthersProto (HO), **6**.

Models at this level have all or some combination of these features and details: grab irons, horns, headlights, antennae, cab sunshades, beacons, windshield wipers, m.u. hoses and cables, etched radiator grills, etched fan grills with fan blades, bells, fuel fillers, fuel gauges, and piping. In many cases these details match specific prototype locomotive road names or numbers, **7**.

Similar to mid-level models, high-end diesels are offered in DC and DCC versions. The DCC models at this level have feature-rich decoders, with prototype-specific sounds (for example, an EMD 567 engine instead of a generic diesel sound or a Nathan K5 air horn instead of a generic horn), lighting effects, and motor control.

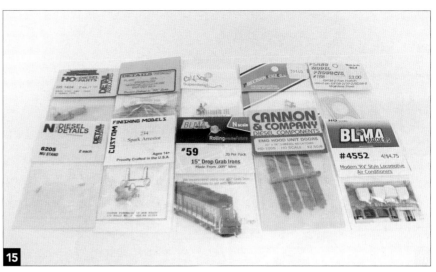

15 Diesel detail parts are available from several companies in N and HO scales.

16 The Fox Valley Models N scale SD70ACe includes painted grab irons and cab sun shades. Dimples make it easy to drill mounting holes for these parts with a pin vise.

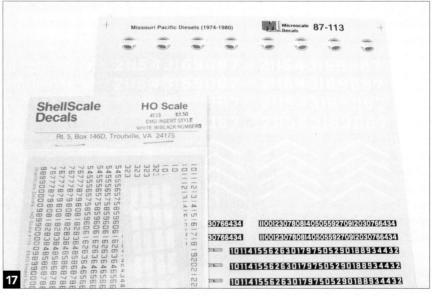

17 Number board decals and number jumbles are available from Microscale, ShellScale Decals, and others.

18

After the number board has been painted and a gloss coat applied, add decal numbers from an appropriate set.

19

The Athearn GP38-2 diesel locomotive at left has a replacement three-chime air horn. The model at right has the stock plastic version that's less detailed.

20

Duratrax R/C Car paint is designed for polycarbonate and other engineering plastics. It works well for painting plastic handrails on diesel locomotives.

Mechanical differences

Externally, HO and N scale diesel models are fairly similar. Most have a plastic body shell with molded or separately applied detail parts, acetal handrails, and knuckle couplers. Under the shell, the models are quite different.

For more than 50 years, Athearn has been using variations of the mechanism shown in **8** on its HO diesels. It features a motor in the center of a die-cast metal frame, a motor with exposed brushes and commutator, and brass flywheels. Universal joints connect the motor to each truck tower. The drive-shaft turns a worm at the top of the truck tower, and the axle gears transfer the motion of the worm to the axles.

Today, most HO locomotives have a weight or weights that span the mechanism, **9**. The wiring for the motor, headlights, and decoder are routed through a printed-circuit (PC) board mounted on top of the weight.

Kato took HO scale mechanism design to a new level when it came out with its HO scale General Electric P42 in 2013. If you look at **10**, you may be wondering where the motor is, as there isn't one in the center of the locomotive. Instead of using a conventional motor, each truck has a coreless motor with a flywheel that drives both axles, **11**. All wheels from each truck pick up track power.

In N scale, split-frame mechanisms have long been the standard, **12**. These mechanisms also have a weight or weights that cover the motor and fly-wheels. A printed-circuit (PC) light board is usually mounted on top the weight, with light-emitting diodes (LEDs) that either directly illuminate the headlights, or clear plastic tubes carry light from the LEDs to the head-lights and, if equipped, ditch lights.

Sound is becoming a common feature on N scale diesels. The mecha-nism from Athearn's Electro-Motive Division F59PHI, **13**, shows how the decoder, speaker, and PC board all fit together in a split-frame mechanism.

Kato broke from the traditional split-frame mechanism with its EMD F40PH, **14**. The mechanism has a one-piece metal frame. Instead of using the frame as an electrical path, phosphor

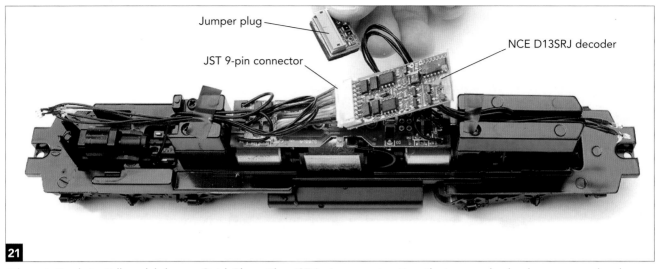

21

Athearn's Ready-to-Roll models have a Quick-Plug with a JST 9-pin connector. Here the jumper plug has been removed and an NCE D13SRJ decoder was installed. The installation is simple and only takes a minute. *Bill Zuback*

Labels on image 21: Jumper plug, JST 9-pin connector, NCE D13SRJ decoder

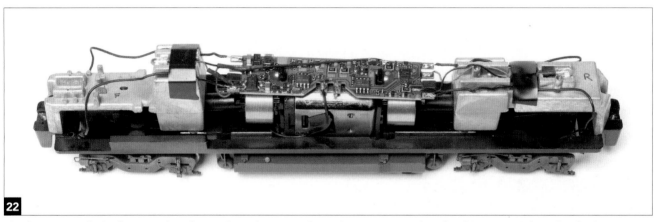

22

The factory-installed 4-function decoder on this Atlas HO scale Dash 8-40B was replaced with a TCS A6X board-style drop-in decoder. Plastic retainers can be used to secure the wires, but solder provides greater reliability. *Jim Forbes*

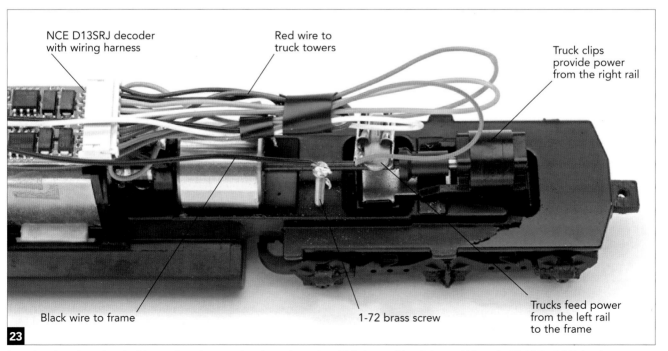

23

Labels on image 23: NCE D13SRJ decoder with wiring harness, Red wire to truck towers, Truck clips provide power from the right rail, Black wire to frame, 1-72 brass screw, Trucks feed power from the left rail to the frame

In some situations, hard-wiring a decoder may be the only option. This is an older Athearn HO scale SD40-2. *Bill Zuback*

24 Unscrewing and removing the draft-gear boxes is all that's required to remove the shell on Athearn Genesis HO scale diesel locomotives. A foam cradle on my workbench protects the model from damage.

Shell-mounting screws

25 On some models, removing the draft-gear box isn't enough. The screws holding this shell on are under the trucks, as on this Rivarossi HO scale U28C.

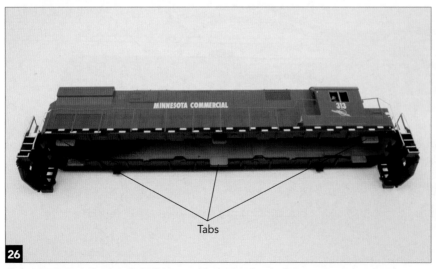

Tabs

26 This Atlas HO scale diesel shell has molded tabs that lock into metal slots on the chassis. The tabs can be released with a thin-bladed standard (flat) screwdriver.

bronze truck contacts transfer current to the PC board.

Detail upgrades

Though many of today's ready-to-run locomotives are well detailed, there are opportunities to enhance them. Fortunately, there are a variety of manufacturers in HO and N scales that produce detail parts, **15**, including BLMA Models (HO and N), Cal-Scale (HO), Cannon & Co. (HO), Custom Finishing Models (HO), Detail Associates (HO and N), Details West, Gold Medal Models (N), Hi-Tech Details (HO), Tichy Train Group (HO), and Utah Pacific (HO).

One of the easiest way to upgrade a model is by adding grab irons and eye bolts, **16**. This can be done with a pin vise, the appropriate drill bit, and formed grab irons. The eye bolts on a model roof simulate lift rings on a real locomotive, which allow hoods to be lifted off the chassis for maintenance.

Though not as common today, some older models may not have printed number boards. This is one of the easiest upgrades you can make, and makes a tremendous improvement on a model. You can use number board decals from Highball Graphics, Microscale, ShellScale, or others, **17**. You can either paint the board the appropriate background color (white or black—check a prototype photo if you're not sure) or use decals. Once the paint has dried or the decal is set, add the numbers, **18**.

Another issue that plagued older models was the use of generic air horns mounted on the cab. As noted in Chapter 4, railroads often have a specific style or two of air horns they like to use. The cab roof was a common horn location, but many railroads (especially in modern times) have moved the placement to the long hood to soften noise for the cab crew.

Adding or changing the horn is usually a simple matter of drilling a new mounting hole, painting the new part, and adding it. Old mounting holes can be filled with plastic putty, the cut-off mounting post of the old horn, or a bit of super glue, with a bit of paint to touch up the area. The models in **19** show the original air horn and the replacement. Other details, such as antennae, bells, and beacons, can be added in similar fashion. Again, check prototype photos for detail style and placement.

Paint can also be used to enhance models. Handrails are one example. Model manufacturers don't always paint the vertical corner handrails a contrasting color, which is usually the case on prototype locomotives. Regular hobby paint works fine on metal handrails, but many new models have acetal plastic handrails. For these, use paint designed for polycarbonate, **20**.

Digital Command Control

Digital Command Control (DCC) has become large part of model railroading. Many newcomers have a lot of questions about the technology, especially when it comes to adding a decoder to a locomotive. If you're just getting started, the easy way is to start with a basic DCC control system and buy locomotives already equipped with DCC decoders. As you gain experience in the hobby, you'll become comfortable working with decoders, programming them, and even adding decoders to non-DCC locomotive models.

If you have a standard DC locomotive with a jumper plug, making the switch to DCC is easy. Just remove the jumper plug, install a compatible decoder, and you're all set, **21**.

Drop-in (plug-and-play) decoders are designed for specific locomotives, **22**. These are designed to be direct replacements for a model's existing PC lighting board, and generally require little, if any, soldering. Installation is generally quite simple; some manufacturers even offer drop-in replacement decoders with sound.

However, drop-in decoders aren't available for every locomotive model. In those cases, hard-wiring a decoder may be necessary, **23**. This requires isolating the motor from the frame, cutting wires, and soldering connections to add a decoder. Check out a book such as *DCC Projects and Applications, Volume 3*, by Mike Polsgrove (Kalmbach Books, 2015), for details on the process. It's not difficult to do, but does

27

The shells on Kato and other N scale models simply slide onto the chassis weight. Carefully pull and wiggle the shell until it slides off—be careful not to damage details.

28

If your model has a large metal weight over the mechanism, you'll need to remove it to access the motor and gear towers.

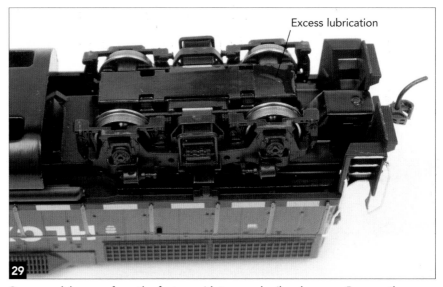

Excess lubrication

29

Some models come from the factory with too much oil and grease. Remove the excess with a soft cloth, or it will attract dirt and dust.

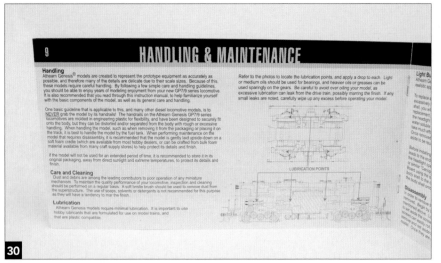

30 Most manufacturers specify where to apply oil and grease to a locomotive, and how often. Make sure the lubricants you use are plastic compatible.

31 A dot of LaBelle no. 106 light grease is all that's needed to lubricate plastic gears. Regular operating will evenly distribute the grease.

32 Metal bearings on the motor, worms, and axles should be lubricated with light oil. LaBelle no. 108 is a popular brand.

require some patience and care. An advantage is that it gives you flexibility in choosing the specific decoder and features that you want.

Several firms offer decoders for HO and N scales, including Digitrax, ESU, Model Rectifier Corp., NCE, QSI Solutions, SoundTraxx, and Train Control Systems. To learn more about DCC, read Larry Puckett's monthly DCC Corner column in *Model Railroader* magazine and books such as *The DCC Guide, 2nd Edition,* by Don Fiehmann (Kalmbach, 2014).

Keeping locomotives running

Today's locomotives are well built and require little maintenance except for lubrication. But there may be occasions where maintenance or a repair require going under the shell.

Manufacturers use a variety of techniques to hold the shell to the mechanism. If possible, check the manufacturer's instructions (most include an exploded diagram). A tip: Keep all the instruction sheets for your locomotives in a common place (folder or three-ring binder) in your workshop or layout room. Many are also available online. These can be quite complex, especially for sound-equipped models.

In HO scale, you often have to remove the coupler (draft-gear) boxes, **24.** Once that's done, the shell may simply lift off, or you may have to remove a few more screws. The screws are typically located near the trucks, **25.** If the shell doesn't lift off that way, check for tabs on the shell that lock on metal lips or slots on the chassis, **26.**

One word of caution with HO models: Headlight wires attached to the PC board may be secured to the shell, and/or the headlights themselves may be secured to the shell behind clear headlight lenses. To avoid breaking the wires or connections, lift the shell off slowly. In N scale, most shells are a press fit and often can be removed without taking off the couplers, **27.** Be sure not to break or bend any details on the shell when doing this.

With the shell removed, you might need to take one more step, and that's removing the weight, **28.**

This will provide access to the motor, truck towers, and other parts that may require maintenance.

Many new locomotives come from the factory with too much lubrication, **29**. If you encounter this, wipe off the excess oil or grease or oil with a soft cloth. Too much lube will attract dust and dirt, actually causing the locomotive to run poorly.

So what areas require oil and grease? That's usually recommended in the paperwork included with the model, **30**. Be sure the oil and grease you apply is plastic compatible. LaBelle no. 106 light grease works well for truck gears, **31**. The same company's no. 108 light oil is suitable for bearings on the motor, worms, and axles, **32**. Remember, a little lubricant goes a long way. A single drop of oil or dot of grease on one gear is all that's necessary. Normal operation will distribute the lubricant evenly.

If you have a locomotive that runs jerkily or makes a lot of noise, check the worm and truck gear covers to make sure they're secured properly, **33**. Also check plastic parts, like truck gears and universal joints, for bits of stray flash (excess plastic from the molding process). Also make sure nothing has gotten in the truck gear housing, like a stray piece of ballast, dirt, or ground foam.

On older models, make sure the commutator and motor brushes are clean. An easy way to clean the commutator is to spin the flywheels by hand and use a pencil eraser to polish the area, **34**. Make sure no residue (rubber bits from the eraser) remains after you do this.

Cleaning wheels

Quite often, a locomotive's poor performance can be chalked up to dirty wheels (and/or dirty track). A quick fix for this is to soak a paper towel with 70 percent isopropyl alcohol and drape it over the rails. Put one truck on the towel, hold the other, and let the locomotive build up some speed. You'll see the grime come off the wheels onto the towel in a few seconds, **35**. Turn the locomotive around and repeat the process. This will work in any scale.

Loose gear cover

If a locomotive runs erratically, make sure the truck and worm gear covers are securely attached. Also check any plastic parts for flash.

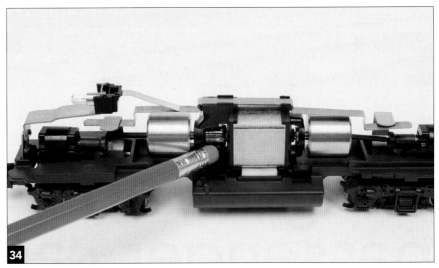
A pencil eraser does a fine job of polishing the commutator on older Athearn diesels. Keep eraser bits from getting in the motor.

Running a locomotive over a paper towel soaked in 70 percent isopropyl alcohol will remove dirt and gunk from the wheels.

1

CHAPTER SIX

Freight and passenger cars

This 40-foot Canadian National boxcar was built in November 1923 and was still in service in the 1970s. The car is single-sheathed (meaning sheathed only on the inside of the truss-style metal bracing) and has wood sides and ends.
Michael Dean, Edmonton Journal

In recent years, the number of freight car models has increased dramatically. Trying to cover every freight and passenger car (model and prototype) from the steam and diesel eras is well beyond the scope of this book. Instead, we'll look at examples of common prototype cars, examine the types of models on the market today, and give you tips on how to enhance your models. We'll also take a brief look at passenger cars, showing you the basic car types and examples of available models.

2 The Pennsylvania Railroad was an early adopter of steel boxcars. The railroad built nearly 30,000 of its class X29 40-foot boxcars. They were the precursor to other standard boxcar designs. *Bud Rothaar*

3 This Great Northern 50-foot boxcar was built in September 1966. As of April 1966, new cars no longer were built with running boards, roof-height ladders, and high-mounted hand brakes. *Staffan Ehnbom*

4 High-cube 86-foot boxcars, such as this former Denver & Rio Grande Western car (now owned by Conrail), are used to haul parts for the automobile industry. *Robert J. Yanosey*

5 This TTX 60-foot boxcar was built by National Steel Car in Canada in 2003. The modern 100-ton excess-height boxcar is used to transport newsprint, pulpboard, asphalt shingles, and many other products.

6 Union Tank Car Co.'s X-3 10,000-gallon tank car was a common steam-era car. It has riveted construction and steel bands that secure the tank to the frame. *Cornelius W. Hauck*

7 A frameless design, no expansion domes, and no side running boards were some of the revolutionary features of this Union car when introduced in 1954. *Union Tank Car Co.*

Boxcars

Boxcars have been the utility player of freight cars for a large part of railroad history. Over the decades, boxcars have been used to haul automobiles, canned goods, building supplies, bagged food, bulk grain, and countless other commodities. In recent decades, items traditionally shipped in boxcars have moved to other cars as well as intermodal containers. Though the number of boxcars has dropped dramatically (450,000 in the 1970s to 116,000 in 2014), they can still be found today serving the food, paper, and auto-parts industries, among others.

Early boxcars, those built from the 1900s through the 1920s, were either of wood or wood-and-steel construction, **1**. Though steel had been used on other freight cars, it wasn't widely used on boxcars until the 1930s. Beginning in the mid-1930s, standard designs adopted by the American Railway Association (ARA) and later the American Association of Railroads (AAR) began being used by multiple

The stenciling and orange commodity panel and number indicate that this modern 100-ton tank car is used in molten sulfur service.

TrinityRail's 30,100-gallon tank car is 59'-5" long. The number on the car's placard (1987) identifies that it is carrying a load of denatured alcohol.

manufacturers and railroads, **2**.

The typical American Association of Railroads (AAR) standard-design boxcar was 40 feet long with a 50-ton capacity and six-foot-wide sliding side doors. They were built by the tens of thousands from the mid-1930s onward, and were the most common freight car into the 1960s. Variations included wider side doors and various styles of ends, roofs, and doors, but they all shared a similar appearance.

By the 1960s, freight cars were becoming more specialized. Longer (50- and 60-foot) cars, many with plug-style doors and internal load restraints, were entering service, **3**.

In 1964, high-cube boxcars arrived on the scene, **4**. These cars, designed to transport automobile parts, were nearly 17 feet tall and 86 feet long. Since the cars were so tall, they weren't required to have running boards (the walkways atop freight car roofs). Two years later, running boards would no longer be required on any new or rebuilt boxcars, refrigerator cars, or stock cars.

In the 1970s, 50-foot boxcars with exterior vertical posts and wider door openings arrived on the scene, many painted yellow for the Railbox pool of cars shared among several railroads, and many for various short lines that operated essentially as car-rental companies. Many of those 50-foot boxcars are still in service today, and while the demand for boxcars isn't as great as in prior decades, new cars are still being constructed, **5**. Common ladings for boxcars today include cases of food products, paper, products in barrels, and packaged goods.

Tank cars

During the steam and early diesel era, tank cars were primarily used by the petroleum industry to transport processed products such as gasoline and fuel oil. Food products were also carried, such as corn oil and other vegetable oils. Cars built from the early 1900s through the 1950s typically had a riveted 8,000- to 12,000-gallon tank and a steel underframe. The tank nested in two saddles, one above each truck, and was secured the car's frame with steel bands, **6**.

In 1954, Union Tank Car Co. debuted a frameless car with the tank providing the strength and serving as the frame, **7**. This car was an innovator in other ways, too, as it featured an all-welded tank and lacked an expansion dome and side running boards. By the

---

Tank car stenciling and lettering

You can often learn the contents of a tank car by looking at its hazmat placard or product identification sticker. But even more information can be gleaned from the classification system used for tank cars, which is stenciled on the side of the car, in this case DOT 111A100W1. What does this code mean?

DOT, or Department of Transportation, is the authorizing agency. You may also see Association of American Railroads (AAR) or Transport Canada (CTC) stenciled here.

111 indicates the class of car, in this case a non-pressurized tank car. Class 103 and 104 tank cars are also non-pressure cars. Pressurized car classes include 105, 112, and 114.

The A is a separator. However, the letters S (tank head protection), T (thermal protection), or J (both types of protection) may be located in this position.

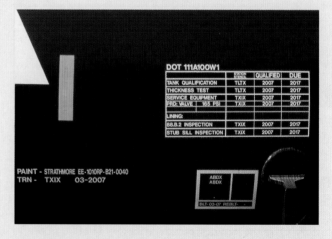

100 is the test pressure of the tank car in psi.

The W indicates fusion-welded construction.

The last 1 is a delineator. It indicates that certain fittings, insulation, tank material, or lining was used.

10

This early 1960s-era Detroit, Toledo & Ironton Pullman-Standard 3,510-cubic-foot-capacity covered hopper is similar in design to the earlier 2,893-cubic-foot-capacity car. *Jim Hediger*

11

Pullman-Standard built two versions of its 4,427-cubic-foot covered hopper. This is the high-side version, which debuted in 1966. It was among the first popular cars for grain service.

12

This Dakota, Minnesota & Eastern car is an example of a Trinity-built 5,161-cubic-foot covered hopper. The 110-ton capacity car is among the most common grain-hauling cars in service today.

13

This steam-era Chicago & North Western 53'-6" flatcar is based on a United States Railroad Administration design. It was modified for trailer-on-flatcar service in the early 1950s. *Chicago & North Western*

14

TTX (formerly Trailer Train Co.) has a large fleet of flatcars designed for many purposes. This bulkhead car is hauling a slab steel load.

15

Grand Trunk Western coil steel car no. 188137, built by National Steel Car, features a one-piece hood to protect the coil steel rolls inside.

1960s, the frameless welded tank was standard, with versions including high-pressure cars for liquified gases.

A push for increased capacity began in the late 1950s and ran through the 1960s, coinciding with increased specialization with cars built to carry certain commodities. In 1970, tank size was capped at 34,500 gallons. Cars can now be found carrying petroleum products, chemicals, acids, food oils and products, clay slurry, molten sulfur, and hundreds of other products.

The design and appearance of today's tank cars is largely driven by the specific commodity they're designed to carry. Examples include the sulfur car in **8** and ethanol car in **9**.

Covered hoppers

Covered hoppers are the most common car type in service today, but they are a relatively recent innovation, with roots dating back only to the 1930s. At that time, several car builders began producing short two-bay 50- and 70-ton cars to carry bulk (powdered) cement, a heavy, dense product requiring protection from the elements. Prior to that, most cement was bagged and carried in boxcars—a very inefficient method. The design was successful, and covered hoppers were soon carrying foundry sand

16

Open-side auto rack cars were common from the 1960s into the 1970s. *Louisville & Nashville*

17

Today's auto racks, like this TTX car with a BNSF rack, are fully enclosed to limit vandalism and other hazards.

18

This Pacific Fruit Express class R-40-20 car is an example of an early steel refrigerator car. PFE was a major operator of reefers through the 1960s. *Trains magazine collection*

19

Mid-century marked the dawn of mechanical refrigerator cars, developed initially to carry frozen foods. This 50-foot car was equipped with roller-bearing trucks. *Santa Fe*

and lime along with cement.

Covered hoppers greatly sped both loading and unloading of bulk products, making up for the fact that they were basically one-commodity cars (and thus would spend half their service lives traveling empty, unlike boxcars, which could be reloaded with something different and sent back on their way).

In the early 1950s, Pullman-Standard unveiled a larger covered hopper, a 2,893-cubic-foot-capacity three-bay car. Railroads began considering the benefits of transporting other granular commodities like sugar, flour, fertilizer, grain, and feed in covered hoppers, **10**. By the 1960s, newer and larger covered hoppers would be used to haul grain, including Pullman-Standard's 100-ton 4,427-cubic-foot-capacity car, **11** (the first popular grain car) and American Car & Foundry's 4,650-cubic-foot-capacity Center Flow. By the early 1970s, covered hop-

pers had taken over most grain traffic, which had been carried in boxcars. Even larger covered hoppers are used for lighter products, such as plastic pellets (used for injection molding) and carbon black.

As early covered hoppers reach the ends of their service lives, they're being replaced with newer, larger cars. One of the most common today is the TrinityRail 5,161-cubic-foot-capacity covered hopper, **12**. Several other manufacturers offer similar cars.

Flatcars

Flatcars have long been used to carry almost any products that were too bulky to fit inside of a boxcar. Common items include machinery, construction/farm equipment, steel beams, pipe, lumber, tanks, and boilers. The majority of steel flatcars from World War I through the 1940s were based on United States Railroad Administration (USRA) and Association of American

Railroads (AAR) designs, **13**, ranging from 42 to 53 feet.

From the 1950s through the 1970s, the General Steel Castings (GSC) 53'-6" Commonwealth flatcar was a popular general-service flatcar. The car was sold as a kit for railroads to build and as a complete car by GSC.

Trailer Train, now TTX, has long operated a large fleet of piggyback and general-service flatcars ranging from 60 to 89 feet, **14**. Examples include 89-foot piggyback and auto-rack flats, bulkhead flatcars, and heavy-duty flats.

Though they may not look the part, coil cars are technically a type of flatcar. Rolls of coiled steel, used to manufacture automobile parts, cans, appliances, and other products, requires protection from the elements. Car builder Evans debuted the first coil car in 1964. An example of a modern coil car is shown in **15**.

Auto racks also fall under the flatcar heading, as the racks that hold vehicles

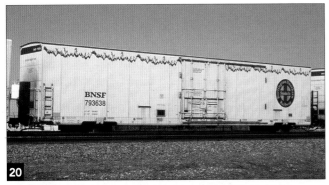

20

This BNSF mechanical reefer is an example of TrinityRail's modern TRINCool 72'-3" car. The car features a satellite system that allows the car's temperature and fuel status to be monitored remotely.

21

Most offset-side hoppers were built to AAR common designs. This two-bay Minneapolis & St. Louis 2,081-cubic-foot-capacity car, built in 1936, is typical of those in service through the 1960s. *Trains magazine collection*

22

These Burlington Northern 100-ton three-bay hoppers were built for unit train service. The white panel indicates the car end with a rotary coupler.

23

Atchison, Topeka & Santa Fe no. 166608 is a 53-foot mill gondola built by American Car & Foundry in 1949. *American Car & Foundry*

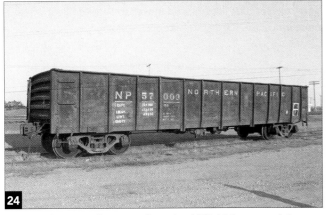

24

This Northern Pacific general-service (GS) 41-foot gondola was used in tie service for its successor Burlington Northern when it was photographed in the mid-1980s. *Steve Grivno photo, Cody Grivno collection*

25

Most of today's gondolas, like this RailGon 66-foot 100-ton car, feature welded construction and straight sills. They carry many products, including scrap metal, wire, pipe, and finished steel components and products.

are attached to long flatcars. Until 1960, autos were carried in 50-foot boxcars, but loading and unloading were cumbersome, and railroads were losing that traffic to trucks. The auto rack earned the traffic back for railroads. Early auto racks had open sides, **16**. However, vandalism led manufacturers to add side panels, roofs, and end doors to the racks. Today's two- and three-deck auto racks are fully enclosed, **17**.

Refrigerator cars

Since their inception, the role of refrigerator cars, or reefers, has been to keep perishable and temperature-sensitive cargo—mainly fruit, vegetables, and meat—cool. Through the 1950s, reefers used ice to keep loads cool, **18**. Bunkers at each end of the car had rooftop hatches to allow loading ice (usually from roof-level platforms) from above. Ice reefers were insulated and they had pairs of swinging side doors. Unlike boxcars, reefers of that period often wore bright

26 Aluminum-bodied bathtub gondolas are used in unit coal train service. Rotary dumpers are used to unload these cars.

27 In the 1950s, existing 40- and 50-foot flatcars were converted for trailer-on-flatcar service. *Illinois Central*

28 The trailer hitches are raised on this 89-foot flatcar. The car also has adjustable pedestals for hauling intermodal containers. *Jeff Wilson*

29 The articulated all-purpose spine car is a lighter alternative than conventional flatcars, and moves trailers and containers more efficiently. *Keith Thompson*

30 This TTX five-unit articulated well car is an example of contemporary intermodal equipment.

31 Kits are not as prevalent as they once were, but a few manufacturers still offer them in HO scale.

colors: Yellow, orange, and red were common, depending upon the owner.

Wood cars were common through the 1930s; Pacific Fruit Express' class R-40-10 reefer marked the beginning of the all-steel reefer era. Many ice-bunker cars remained in service through the 1960s, but by the early 1970s, they were gone—replaced by mechanical refrigerator cars (or trucks).

Reefers with mechanical refrigeration units began appearing in the 1950s, **19**. They were initially developed for the emerging frozen-food business. Their high price limited them to that service into the 1960s, when mechanical reefers began seeing use in produce and meat service as well, although those commodities were largely moving to trucks.

Though there were some 40-foot mechanical refrigerator cars (primarily converted ice-bunker cars), most were 50- and 60-foot cars.

A subset of refrigerator cars is the insulated boxcar. While these cars lack ice or mechanical refrigeration, they can keep items that are cooled before loading at a stable temperature for multiple days. The cars have an

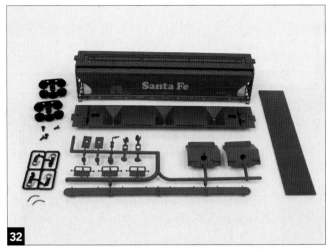

32

Accurail's HO scale ACF 4,600-cubic-foot Center Flow covered hopper is an easy-to-build plastic kit. Building kits like this is a great way to develop modeling skills.

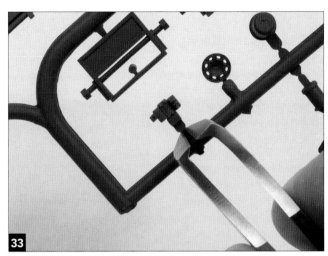

33

Carefully remove plastic parts from their sprues with sprue-cutting tweezers. Flush sprue cutters may be necessary for larger parts.

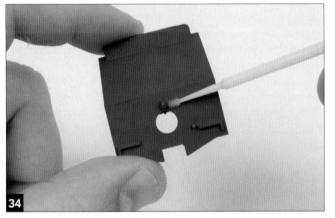

34

Use liquid plastic cement to attach parts to the model. For best results, apply the glue from an inconspicuous location, such as the underbody.

35

Once body details have been added, attach the shell to the underbody. On this car, small lips on the car ends will hold the weight in place.

36

Here is the finished Accurail covered hopper. Simple kits like these make fun evening projects.

37

This HO scale WalthersTrainline car features basic details and simplified painting and lettering.

Association of American Railroads designation of RBL, which stands for refrigerated, bunkerless, with load-restraining devices. They began appearing in large numbers in the 1960s, as new types of foam insulation made cars much more efficient at holding temperatures constant.

Mechanical reefers and insulated boxcars from the 1960s and 1970s can still be found in service, along with new, larger mechanical reefers, **20**.

Hoppers

Some of the earliest all-steel cars were hoppers and gondolas. The basic design of the hopper hasn't changed much since the early 20th century: sloped interiors that lead to two, three, or more doors at the bottom of the car. Hopper cars are used to transport bulk commodities that aren't weather sensitive, mainly coal but also gravel and other aggregates.

Freight car lettering

Freight cars have a variety of lettering. Here is what all of the lettering means on this Soo Line car in 1980.
Jim Hediger

1) Road name and/or herald or slogan. This isn't required.

2) Reporting marks. These are required on all cars. Every owner is assigned its own set of initials (some large railroads have multiple marks, including those of predecessor lines). An "X" at the end means the car is privately owned.

3) Road number. This is also required. Only one car can have this number per reporting mark.

4) Capacity. The car's capacity in pounds. This hasn't been required on new cars since 1985. This line is often painted out on older cars.

5) Load limit. The maximum weight of the load itself.

6) Light weight. The weight of the car when empty.

7) AAR mechanical designation. This car's designation is XM, which indicates a general-service boxcar

8) Built date. The data is now in the consolidated panel.

9) Dimensional data. For boxcars and refrigerator cars, the internal and external dimensions of the car.

10) Consolidated stencil. These date to 1972. The panels document axle and brake maintenance.

11) Tack boards. On some modern cars, they're only on the ends. Some cars have them on the sides, either on the body or the doors. Smaller boards are route boards.

12) Automatic Car Identification (ACI) label. This barcode-style system, used from 1967 to 1977, proved unreliable as grime made labels unreadable. Newer cars (since 1994) have an Automatic Equipment

Identification tag, a small box located at the bottom of each car side. Trackside scanners read these non-optical tags.

13) U1 inspection label. In March 1978, all cars were to be inspected for a specific manufacturer's wheel that was linked to several derailments. Cars without the wheels received a 6" yellow dot in a 9" black square. Cars with the wheels in question received white dots.

The USRA 50-ton two-bay hopper was among the earliest mass-produced hoppers, with more than 25,000 constructed. By the late 1920s, hoppers evolved to an offset-side design, with the side steel sheathing outside of vertical posts, with sheathing slanting inward at the top of the sides.

Offset-side hoppers were common from the 1920s to the 1950s, **21**. Two-bay versions of the car had 50- and 55-ton capacities. The three- and four-bay versions were rated at 70 tons.

The shift from loose-car customers, like small-town fuel dealers, local municipal power plants, and small businesses and industries, to large coal-powered electrical utilities during the 1960s and 1970s, had an impact on hopper design. During this time, more than a half dozen car builders were manufacturing 100-ton capacity

hoppers, **22**. Many of these cars were used in unit trains (a solid train bound for a single destination).

Widespread use of aluminum-body coal hoppers started in the 1980s and continues today. These cars are owned by major railroads and electric utilities. Although many unit trains have shifted to large gondolas, many hoppers can still be found in coal service.

Gondolas

Gondolas were often used to haul coal in the steam era. Over the years, they've also been called on to haul rock, scrap metal, finished metal products, coil steel, wood chips, and bulky items that don't fit in boxcars.

The two most common categories of gondolas during the steam and early diesel eras were mill and general service. Mill gondolas are at least 50

feet long, with low sides, and they often have drop ends (end doors that fold down into the car), **23**. These cars mainly served steel mills.

General service (GS) cars were shorter and had higher sides, **24**. Many general-service gondolas had drop bottoms to facilitate unloading. They could haul bulky objects or bulk commodities like coal, coke, and sand.

Like boxcars, pre-World War I gondolas featured wood sides and steel bracing. After the war, all-steel gondolas became more common. Following World War II and into the 1950s, typical car lengths were 53 to 65 feet.

Welded gondolas have been around since the 1960s. The design has evolved over the years, with today's straight side-sill 100-ton cars being the most common, **25**.

38

Athearn's HO scale Ready-to-Roll line is an example of a mid-level factory-assembled car. This FMC 4,700-cubic-foot-capacity covered hopper features separately applied details, metal wheelsets, metal running boards, and plastic knuckle couplers.

39

Molco's HO scale Atchison, Topeka & Santa Fe class Bx-94 boxcar has many separately applied detail parts, metal wheelsets, and Kadee knuckle couplers.

40

Some resin kits, such as this Rail Yard Models (now out of production) HO scale Pullman-Standard covered hopper, include plastic and etched-brass detail parts. *Jim Forbes*

41

This Winston-Salem Southbound caboose was built from an American Model Builders HO scale wood kit. Most wood kits don't include trucks or couplers.

42

Using Microscale's Micro Sol and Scotch Magic tape, I was able to remove factory lettering from an Athearn car. This trick may not work on cars from other manufacturers.

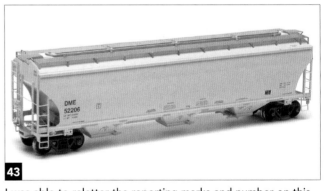

43

I was able to reletter the reporting marks and number on this covered hopper for the Dakota, Minnesota & Eastern without having to repaint the car.

In a case of what's old is new again, gondolas became the car of choice for coal hauling from the 1980s onward. Rotary dumpers at power plants—together with rotary couplers on coal cars—made it possible to quickly and easily unload gondolas. Like hoppers, most early 100-ton cars featured steel construction, while new cars commonly have aluminum bodies, **26**.

Intermodal equipment

Intermodal means traffic that moves by more than one type of transportation. For railroads, this means truck trailers that also ride on flatcars and containers that can be moved among railcars, truck chassis, and ships. While we often think of intermodal as a modern aspect of railroading, extensive use of trailer-on-flatcar (TOFC) dates

back to the 1930s. In early days, most TOFC (piggyback) traffic was handled on existing 40- and 50-foot flatcars, **27**.

As longer trailers were built, longer flatcars were required to accommodate two trailers per flatcar. By 1960, the 89-foot flatcar was standard for this, built by Bethlehem, American Car & Foundry, and Pullman-Standard, **28**. Intermodal containers began appearing

44

Andy Sperandeo used decals to add chalk marks and update the reweigh and repack data on this ExactRail HO scale boxcar for his 1940s-era layout.

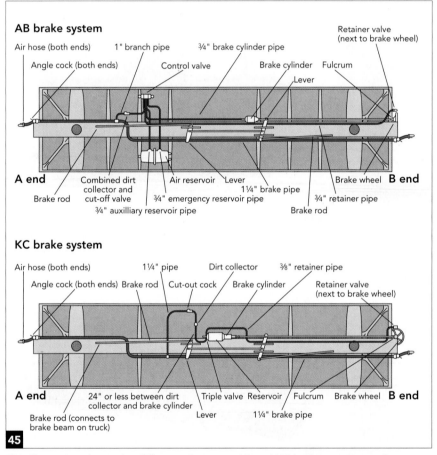

AB brake system

Air hose (both ends) 1" branch pipe ¾" brake cylinder pipe Retainer valve (next to brake wheel)
Angle cock (both ends) Control valve Brake cylinder Fulcrum
Lever

A end
Combined dirt collector and cut-off valve Air reservoir Lever Brake wheel **B end**
Brake rod 1¼" brake pipe ¾" retainer pipe
¾" emergency reservoir pipe Brake rod
¾" auxilliary reservoir pipe

KC brake system

Air hose (both ends) 1¼" pipe Dirt collector ⅜" retainer pipe
Angle cock (both ends) Brake rod Cut-out cock Brake cylinder Retainer valve (next to brake wheel)

A end
24" or less between dirt collector and brake cylinder Triple valve Reservoir Fulcrum Brake wheel **B end**
Brake rod (connects to brake beam on truck) Lever 1¼" brake pipe

45

This illustration shows the difference between AB and KC brake systems on boxcar underbodies. Component placement varies by car type.

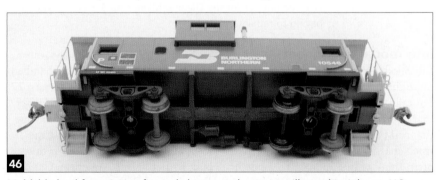

46

Moldable lead from A-Line fit nicely between the center sills on this Athearn HO scale caboose. The weight isn't visible when the car is on the track.

in large numbers by the early 1970s. To accommodate trailers and containers, 89-foot cars were built with adjustable container pedestals and collapsible fifth-wheel hitches.

Another innovation of the intermodal era was the all-purpose spine car, **29**. As the name suggests, the car is basically a spine/center sill with platforms to support trailer wheels and hitch or container mounting levers.

Containers now dominate intermodal traffic, carried mainly in double-stack well cars, **30**. Southern Pacific and Sea-Train started testing single- and three-unit well cars in 1977, and a five-unit articulated production car appeared in 1981. Soon after, several car builders and railroads began building and buying similar cars.

Modern double-stack cars can be found as single cars and three-unit articulated sets with 53-foot wells to accommodate 53-foot (and shorter 45-, 40-, and 20-foot) containers, and five-unit sets of 40-foot wells. Containers are stacked and locked in place by inter-box connectors (IBCs). Container locking slots are at the corners of 20- and 40-foot containers, and inset from the ends of longer containers so they mate at the 40-foot position.

Freight car models

There are a variety of models on the market today in assembled and unassembled versions. Though not as prevalent as they once were, injection-molded plastic kits are still on the market. Accurail, Bowser, Con-Cor, Kadee, and ScaleTrains.com are among the contemporary manufacturers of HO scale kits, **31**. Athearn and Model Die Casting (Roundhouse) kits, though out of production, were longtime staples of the hobby and—along with kits from other manufacturers—are still plentiful at swap meets and online auction websites like eBay.

Basic kits are a great way to develop modeling skills, **32**. The first thing I do when building a kit is make a visual inspection. Are all of the parts included? Are all of the parts in good shape?

Next, following the directions, carefully cut parts from their sprues, **33**.

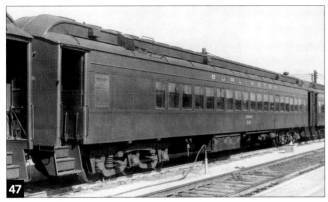

47 Chicago, Burlington & Quincy cafe-coach no. 351 is an example of a heavyweight car. It has a clerestory roof (raised down the middle) and six-wheel trucks. *Jim C. Seacrest*

48 Southern Railway coach no. 834 is a lightweight streamlined car that was built by American Car & Foundry in July 1950. *American Car & Foundry*

49 Sleeping cars came in a variety of configurations, identifiable often by window arrangement. This Atchison, Topeka & Santa Fe car has 4 bedrooms, 4 compartments, and 2 drawing rooms. *American Car & Foundry*

50 This streamlined lightweight Southern diner-lounge car had less table seating than a traditional diner. The kitchen is at the right end of the car. *American Car & Foundry*

51 Observation cars were designed for the ends of trains. One of the more recognizable observation cars was Milwaukee Road's Skytop Lounge. It's shown here on the 1948 *Twin Cities Hiawatha*. *Milwaukee Road*

52 The catcher arm over the left door on this Norfolk & Western Railway Post Office car would catch mail pouches hung from trackside mail cranes. Clerks sorted mail in RPO cars while in transit. *Trains magazine collection*

Then attach any separately applied parts (on this car, the hatch cover, outlet gates, brake appliances, and brake wheel) with liquid plastic cement, **34**.

Then set the weight in place, insert the car ends, and attach the body to the underframe, **35**. Finally, install the trucks and couplers and check them against a National Model Railroad Association standards gauge (see Chapters 7 and 8). If they check out,

your car is ready for service, **36**.

The vast majority of today's HO and N scale freight cars are ready-to-run. However, not all ready-to-run cars are the same, as they vary in level of detail. Examples of basic ready-to-run cars include Athearn's contemporary Roundhouse line (HO), the Atlas Trainman line (HO and N), Bachmann's Silver Series (HO and N), Con-Cor (HO and N),

InterMountain's Value Line (HO), and WalthersTrainline (HO). Most of these cars have molded-on details with few, if any, separately applied parts, **37**. They typically have plastic knuckle couplers.

Mid-level cars make up the bulk of the ready-to-run market. Examples include Athearn's Ready-to-Roll line (HO), the Atlas Master Line (HO and N), Bluford Shops (N), Bowser (HO and N), Broadway Limited (HO and

53

A detailed, multi-color plastic interior is just one of the many highlights of this Walthers HO scale Pullman heavyweight sleeping car. *Jim Forbes*

54

Rapido Trains raised the bar with its HO scale injection-molded plastic sleeper and coach. The models feature more than 100 parts, including many underbody details. *Jim Forbes*

55

Micro-Trains has produced a variety of heavyweight passenger cars in N scale. Models have accurate paint schemes, lots of detail, and most of the models have plastic interiors. *Bill Zuback*

N), Micro-Trains (N), the Operator line from ScaleTrains.com, and WalthersMainline (HO). At minimum these cars have some separately applied parts (or provisions for adding them) and metal wheelsets, **38**.

Top-of-the-line models include BLMA (HO and N), Fox Valley Models (HO and N), Kadee (HO), Moloco (HO), Rapido Trains (HO and N), ScaleTrains.com's Rivet Counter line (HO), Tangent Scale Models (HO), and WalthersProto (HO). These cars feature prototype-specific paint schemes and detailing and many separately applied detail parts, **39**.

Sometimes a specific prototype car isn't available as a plastic kit or ready-to-run model. Many models of more-obscure prototypes are available as cast-resin kits in HO and N scales. Manufacturers include Funaro & Camerlengo, Westerfield, and Wright Trak Railroad Models, among many others.

Resin kits vary in complexity, but most are more involved than plastic kits, and they need to be painted and decaled by the modeler. Some have one-piece bodies, while others have to be assembled from flat molded parts. Be aware that most resin kits do not include trucks, wheelsets, couplers, or weights. However, some do include finely rendered etched-brass and plastic details that further enhance the model, **40**. It's usually a good idea to gain some other model-building experience before taking on a resin kit.

Wood kits, common in the hobby's infancy, are still around and are better than ever. American Model Builders makes laser-cut, prototype-specific wood caboose kits in HO and N scales, **41**. The kits feature tab-and-slot construction, peel-and-stick parts, separate step castings, and brake detail. Kits require painting; modeler-supplied parts include trucks, couplers, detail parts, and decals.

Model upgrades

Just because a car is ready to run does not mean it can't be further enhanced. For example, I had a gray Athearn HO scale Ready-to-Roll covered hopper lettered for Coors Brewing Co. I didn't have a need for the car as decorated. Instead, I removed the lettering with Microscale Micro Sol and Scotch Magic tape, **42**. I then sprayed the car with clear gloss and relettered it with assorted Microscale decals, **43**.

On older cars, updating the reweigh and repacking information and adding chalk marks can make an out-of-the-box model really stand out, **44**.

Try to avoid anachronistic details on your models. Don't use cast-iron wheels with ribbed backs on modern freight cars (see Chapter 8). Make sure the brake system is correct for the model. AB brakes started being used in 1933. Older K-style brakes (KC and KD) were banned from interchange service on July 1, 1953, **45**.

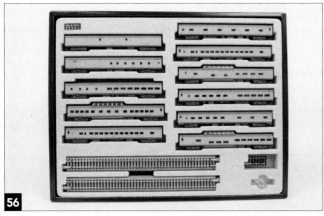

56

Kato is one of a handful of manufacturers that offer complete name trains. Here is the manufacturer's N scale Union Pacific *City of Los Angeles.*

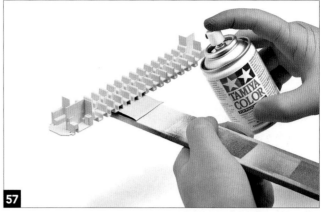

57

Model paint doesn't stick well to acetal, a slippery engineering plastic used on many passenger car interiors. A primer coat of Tamiya for Polycarbonate will solve that problem. *Bill Zuback*

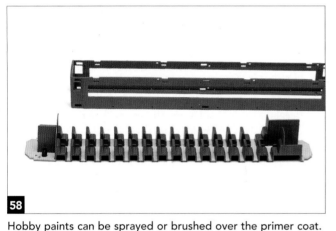

58

Hobby paints can be sprayed or brushed over the primer coat. This looks much better than the solid piece of tan plastic, doesn't it? *Bill Zuback*

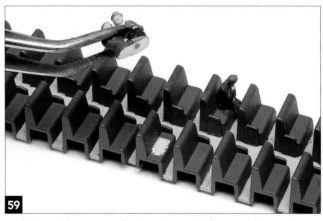

59

With the wide variety of HO and N scale figures, there's no reason not to put a few inside your passenger cars. Viewers won't notice the missing legs. *Bill Zuback*

Lastly, make sure your freight cars are the proper weight to ensure trouble-free operation. The National Model Railroad Association (NMRA) has a recommended practice (RP20.1) for weighting cars. Having cars with consistent weights avoids having lighter cars that can tip on curves when placed ahead of heavier cars in trains.

The NMRA's formula for HO scale cars is an initial weight of 1 ounce plus .5 ounce per inch of car length. Thus, a 50-foot car (about 7 inches) should weigh 1 + (7 x .5) or 4.5 ounces.

In N scale, the formula is an initial weight of .5 ounce plus .15 ounce per inch of length.

When building a kit, install the weight before assembly. A-Line and Adair Shops are a two sources for weights designed for model railroading. Peel-and-stick lead weights, moldable lead, and pourable lead are some options on the market, **46**. Car kits often include sheet-steel weights.

Lead sheet, pennies, and BBs can also be used. Make sure you wash your hands thoroughly after handling lead.

Prototype passenger cars

Passenger cars are typically longer than freight cars (60 to 80 feet) and fall into two broad categories: heavyweight, **47**, and lightweight cars, **48**. Built through the 1930s, standard steel passenger cars were indeed heavy, and often rode on six-wheel trucks.

The introduction of new streamlined trains beginning in the 1930s brought new construction techniques, including fluted stainless-steel sides or thin aluminum sheet over lightweight frames. This resulted in substantial weight savings (often 10 to 20 tons per car). The new lightweight cars often rode on four-wheel trucks.

The most common passenger car is the coach or chair car, **48**. The general arrangement is two-by-two seating on each side of a center aisle. Rigid-back seats packed closer together are common on short-distance and commuter coaches. Coach seats on long-distance trains are spaced farther apart, can recline, and have leg rests.

For passengers traveling overnight or long distances, sleeping cars provide the best accommodations. Sleepers were built to hundreds of different patterns, with various sizes and types of rooms and accomodations. The Atchison, Topeka & Santa Fe car in **49** is a 4-bedroom, 4-compartment, 2-drawing-room sleeper built by American Car & Foundry. A drawing room is a large room with a private bathroom and berths for three passengers. A compartment is also private but lacks its own bathroom.

Adding grab irons is easy, especially if the car has drill starter points, like this WalthersMainline HO scale sleeper.

A strip of .030" styrene ensures that the grab irons are properly spaced from the model. Remove it when the glue dries.

Dining cars typically featured a kitchen or galley in part of the car and seating for 36 to 48 passengers in the rest. On trains with fewer passengers or shorter routes, a diner-lounge might be used instead, **50**. The lounge was on the opposite end of the car from the kitchen.

Observation cars were often the signature car on premiere "name" trains. These cars let passengers sit in comfortable seats and take in the passing landscape. Many observation cars featured round or boat-tail ends, and often the design was unique to the railroad, such as those on the Milwaukee Road, **51**.

Railway Post Office cars carried mail on the rails from the steam era through the 1960s, **52**. Postal clerks from the United States Postal Service's Railway Mail Service division rode these cars, receiving and sorting mail while the train was in motion. A catcher arm would grab mail pouches hung on trackside mail cranes. Mailbags for towns along the line were either kicked off or thrown from RPO cars onto station platforms.

Baggage cars, as their name implies, carried checked baggage for passengers. However, the cars were more than that. Their main job was carrying parcels and shipments for the Railway Express Agency, which was essentially the United Parcel Service of the steam and early diesel eras. Storage mail (mail not sorted en route) was kept in sealed pouches in baggage cars.

Passenger car models

Passenger car models have evolved greatly over the years. Many early HO scale kits had embossed steel sides, wood or plastic roofs, wood floors, metal detail castings, and decals.

Today's HO scale models are much improved. Manufacturers include Athearn (Genesis series and Roundhouse line), Atlas (former Branchline Trains models), Bachmann, Broadway Limited, Centralia Car Shops, Con-Cor, Fox Valley Models, Kato, Mantua, MTH Electric Trains, Rivarossi, and Walthers.

Kits and car sides are available from American Model Builders, Brass Car Sides, Eastern Car Works, Funaro & Camerlengo, JJL Models, La Belle Woodworking Co., Laser Horizons, NKP Car Sides, Train Station Products, and Union Station Products, among others.

Walthers, Rivarossi, and a few others use applique sides that press-fit on a core body. Some of the Walthers cars have painted plastic interiors, **53**, while others are molded in a single color.

Rapido Trains, a Canadian-based manufacturer (not to be confused with older N scale couplers), offers high-end passenger cars in HO and N scales. The injection-molded plastic HO scale cars shown in **54** feature more than 100 individually applied parts, battery-operated light-emitting diode interior lighting controlled with a magnetic reed switcher, and removable markers.

In N scale, passenger cars are produced by Bachmann, Centralia Car Shops, Con-Cor, Fox Valley Models, Kato, Micro-Trains, Rapido Trains, and Wheels of Time, **55**. Kits and car sides are offered by American Model Builders, Brass Car Sides, Eastern Seaboard Models Corp., Fine N Scale, JnJ Trains, M&R Car Sides, NKP Car Sides, TR Hobby Products, and Union Station Products.

Modeling complete passenger trains piecemeal in both scales is possible thanks to the many cars available in both scales. However, companies like Con-Cor, Fox Valley Models, Kato, Rapido Trains, and Walthers make the job easier by offering various complete name trains, **56**. Some companies only offer the cars, while others offer everything from the locomotives to the observation car.

Passenger car upgrades

Though many contemporary cars are well detailed, there are plenty of options for adding exterior details. In HO scale, American Limited Models, Athabasca Scale Models, Bethlehem Car Works, The Coach Yard, Eastern Car Works, Great Western Passenger Car Details, Hi-Tech Details, New England Rail Services, Palace Car Co., Red Cap Line, Tomar Industries, Train Station Products, and Walthers offer detail parts. In N, American Limited Models, Athabasca, JnJ Trains, M&R Car Sides, Palace, Rapido, and Tomar offer details.

62

Buzz Lenander tinted the windows of his N scale Atchison, Topeka & Santa Fe *El Capitan* cars with Top Flite's MonoKote Metallic Green film. The product is designed for model airplanes, but it effectively captures the blue-green appearance of glazing used on many passenger cars.

63

Two coats of Model Master Lusterless Flat (the aerosol can version) effectively frosted the lavatory windows on this HO scale Rivarossi coach.

64

This WalthersMainline 85-foot passenger car, left, has coupler arms connected to the trucks. Upgrade kits, right, with metal trucks and body-mounted couplers, are available.

65

Andy Sperandeo body-mounted Kadee no. 5 couplers on his passenger cars, which run on broad curves. He set the draft-gear boxes back for close coupling between cars. *Jim Forbes*

You can do several things to upgrade passenger cars. Start with interior paint and figures. A few years ago I upgraded some Rivarossi HO scale 60-foot coaches for a *Model Railroader* project layout. I started by priming the one-piece plastic interior with Taimya Color for Polycarbonate, **57**. This paint sticks well to acetal plastic, and model paints can be applied on top of it.

I airbrushed the floor with Model Master Acrylic Tan, the seats Acrylicos Vallejo Calvary Brown, and the walls and core Acrylicos Vallejo Mahogany Brown, **58** (brush-painting also works).

I added an assortment of figures from Prieser. To ensure strong bonds, I scraped paint from the gluing faces, **59**.

You can show off all that hard work by lighting the car's interior. Light kits for standard DC and Digital Command Control are available from

Walthers. Battery-operated units controlled by a magnetic reed switch are offered in HO and N scales by Rapido Trains and Fox Valley Models.

Though many cars come with factory-installed wire grab irons, some don't. However, the cars that lack grab irons often have drill-starter points, which make it easy to drill the openings with a pin vise, **60**. Dip the grab irons in cyanoacrylate adhesive and press them into place, using a piece of .030" styrene strip as a spacer, **61**.

Many passenger cars had tinted windows or frosted windows. When Buzz Lenander was modeling the Atchison, Topeka & Santa Fe's *El Capitan* in N scale, he used MonoKote Metallic Green to tint the windows, **62**. The product, produced by Top Flite, is a transparent film often used by airplane modelers.

Going back to the Rivarossi coach from earlier, the bathroom windows had clear glazing, which didn't give the HO passengers much privacy. I sprayed the inside of the window glazing with Model Master Lusterless Flat, which gives the glass a frosted look, **63**.

Today's modelers are blessed with an abundance of scale-length passenger cars. However, these require broad-radius curves (at least 22" radius). To remedy that, some manufacturers offer passenger cars with couplers mounted on arms connected to the trucks, couplers with long shanks, or special draft-gear boxes that provide extra coupler swing, **64**. However, long passenger cars still look their best on broad curves. If your layout has 30" radius or broader curves, consider body-mounting couplers, **65**. Test a couple of cars before equipping your entire fleet.

1

CHAPTER SEVEN

Prototype and model couplers

This company service flatcar has Type E knuckle couplers. Variations of this coupler have been used on freight cars and locomotives since the early 1930s. The horizontal rod extending under the coupler to the left is the uncoupling lever. Pulling the lever handle (left) upward opens the coupler knuckle.

Although small, couplers play a big role in smooth, reliable operation. If couplers function properly and are installed per the manufacturer's instructions, you should have few, if any, problems. We'll explore the HO and N scale couplers on the market today, help you pick the right ones for your locomotives and freight cars, and show you how to install and fine-tune them for hours of operational enjoyment.

2
The Type E lower-shelf coupler lacks the alignment wings of its Type F interlocking cousin.

3
Double-shelf couplers are mandatory on tank cars carrying hazardous materials.

4
Horn-hook couplers were standard on HO scale train set models and freight cars kits for decades. Today—thank goodness—few manufacturers use them. *Jim Forbes*

5
Kadee's Magne-Matic automatic knuckle coupler has been the *de facto* hobby standard for many years. This is an example of the company's HO scale no. 5 coupler. *Jim Forbes*

6
Weathering knuckle couplers greatly enhances their realism. Painting the trip pin grimy black and coloring the tip with a silver paint marker simulates an air hose and metal glad hand. *Jim Forbes*

Prototype couplers

Knuckle couplers have been used on prototype equipment since the late 1890s. The first "standard" coupler adopted by the Association of American Railroads (AAR) was the Type E, **1**. Many improvements have been made to the coupler since its debut in 1930. Except for tank cars, the standard Type E coupler continues to be used on a variety of freight cars.

Type F interlocking couplers date back to the late 1940s, and became an AAR alternate standard on freight cars in 1954. The couplers feature a bottom shelf and alignment wings designed to support an adjacent coupler should it pull out. This helps prevent cars from uncoupling during a derailment. Today, Type F interlocking couplers are commonly found on cars designed for unloading in a rotary dumper. Type E lower-shelf couplers, which lack alignment wings, date back to the late 1960s. They're found on boxcars and covered hoppers, among other cars, **2**.

Today, all tank cars interchanged between railroads have been equipped with double-shelf couplers, **3**. The Type F interlocking coupler was first mandated on hazardous material cars in 1970. By the late 1970s, the AAR mandated new and rebuilt tank cars be equipped with double-shelf couplers. The purpose of the double-shelf design is to keep cars coupled in a derailment, preventing an adjacent coupler from riding up and puncturing the neighboring tank car head.

7

The HO Kadee no. 148 coupler features wire ("whisker") centering springs, eliminating the need for a separate phosphor bronze centering spring.
Bill Zuback

8

Accurail, McHenry (Athearn), Life-Like, and Bachmann are among the manufacturers of plastic knuckle couplers. The couplers are molded in black or brown engineering plastic.

9

Recent additions to the HO metal coupler market include Rapido Trains (MacDonald Cartier) and Wm. K. Walthers (Proto-Max).

10

MTH Electric Trains sells HO scale locomotives with remote-control couplers. The couplers can be activated with Digital Command Control or MTH's proprietary Digital Command System.
Bill Zuback

11

Scale-size HO couplers are offered by Accurail, Kadee, McHenry (Athearn), and Sergent Engineering. Those made by Kadee and McHenry are compatible with standard couplers, while those from Accurail and Sergent Engineering aren't.

12

Lower-shelf and double-shelf couplers are produced in HO by Kadee and McHenry. As with each firm's standard couplers, Kadee's couplers are metal and McHenry's are plastic.

The evolution of HO scale couplers

When HO scale was in its early years, rolling stock featured either manufacturer-specific couplers or lacked couplers completely. In the latter situation, it was up to the modeler to select and install couplers.

By comparison, today's HO scale model railroaders have it much easier. Virtually all locomotives and freight cars are equipped with some brand of operating knuckle couplers, most of which work with each other. But into the 1990s, horn-hook couplers were the standard on almost all locomotives and freight cars, **4**. Manufacturers liked horn-hook couplers because they were inexpensive to make (there were no moving parts) and the design could be used without charge.

While horn-hooks are easy to couple, they have a couple of major drawbacks. First is their appearance:

They are ugly. Horn-hook couplers look nothing like couplers found on full-size locomotives and freight cars. Horn-hooks detract from otherwise well-proportioned, detailed, and painted models.

When it comes to operations, horn-hook couplers have problems, too. They are difficult to uncouple by hand, and they can't be uncoupled automatically. If the couplers are truck mounted, as often the case on train-set and entry-level models, side forces while cuts of cars are being pushed tend to skew the trucks, which can lead to derailments (especially on curves).

The Kadee revolution

An alternative debuted in 1953 when brothers Dale and Keith Edwards introduced their first Kadee knuckle coupler. Seven years later, the duo unveiled the Kadee Magne-Matic coupler, **5**. The new coupler looked

more like the real thing, operated well, and was easy to install. The Kadee coupler quickly grew in popularity with modelers, and is the *de facto* standard in the hobby. For many years Kadee couplers were only available as aftermarket products. Today, they're featured on high-end models from ExactRail, Moloco, and Tangent Scale Models, among others.

Magne-Matic couplers are made of cast zinc alloy and feature a bronze coil knuckle spring. The trip pin is made of soft iron. A small lip cast on the inside of the knuckle prevents the couplers from separating when passing over an uncoupling magnet.

Some modelers remove the trip pin and install separate aftermarket air hoses on their models for a more prototypical appearance. However, this means uncoupling can only be done manually, as the trip pin is necessary to spread the couplers apart over a

13 Rapido couplers are the horn-hooks of the N scale world. The couplers were standard on rolling stock into the 1990s. *Bill Zuback*

14 Kadee debuted its N scale Magne-Matic coupler in the late 1960s. It's been the choice of serious N scale modelers for decades.

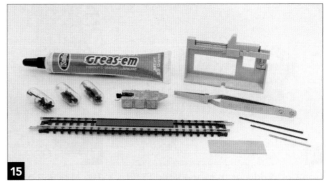

15 A great way to learn the Magne-Matic system is with Micro-Trains' N scale coupler starter set. Item no. 1059 includes coupler conversions, a coupler assembly jig, trip pin and coupler height gauges, and a drill-and-tap set, among other items.

16 New N scale knuckle couplers appeared on the market after the Kadee (Micro-Trains) patents began to expire. From left are Accurail (Accumate, used on Atlas models), Bachmann (E-Z Mate), and McHenry (Athearn).

17 Kato knuckle couplers are used on the firm's N scale locomotives, freight, and passenger cars. The trip pin is installed by the modeler. *Jim Forbes*

magnet. Others paint the trip pin black or dark gray to simulate an air hose, **6**.

Though Kadee has a robust lineup of dozens of coupler models, the most popular has long been the no. 5. It features a ⁹⁄₃₂" shank (the distance from the center of the mounting pin to the back of the knuckle head) and a bronze centering spring. The no. 5 coupler fits with little or no modification in coupler boxes on most freight car models from Accurail, Athearn, Bowser, and Walthers, among others.

A fairly recent development is Kadee's line of "whisker" couplers. The all-metal couplers have thin built-in centering springs on the shank, eliminating the need for the separate phosphor-bronze springs used on standard Kadee couplers. The hole in

the shank is designed to fit around the ⅛" boss in most draft-gear boxes. The no. 148, **7**, is the whisker equivalent of a no. 5 coupler.

The Kadee coupler line is explained in detail in the firm's 52-page catalog and on its website, www.kadee.com. If you do a lot of freight-car modeling, you'll find it handy to get sampler test kit no. 13, which includes one each of the no. 5, 20- and 30-series insulated couplers (these feature plastic shanks and cast-metal knuckles to prevent short circuits), standard and scale whisker couplers, draft-gear boxes, springs, and uncouplers.

The next generation
When Kadee's original patents expired, a new crop of knuckle couplers from

several manufacturers joined the market beginning in the late 1990s. Most of these couplers were designed to operate with Kadee couplers.

Plastic knuckle couplers have been produced by Accurail (Accumate), Bachmann (E-Z Mate), Life-Like, and McHenry, **8**. The couplers are made of tough engineering plastic with, depending on the manufacturer, a one- or two-piece design and plastic or coil metal knuckle springs.

Metal couplers are offered by Rapido Trains (MacDonald Cartier) and Wm. K. Walthers (Proto-Max), **9**. Rapido couplers can be found on the firm's locomotives, freight cars, and passenger cars. The Proto-Max couplers are used on WalthersProto and WalthersMainline cars. Both brands,

18

Con-Cor produces truck-mounted Rigid Jaw couplers. The couplers are well-suited for unit trains that don't require frequent uncoupling.

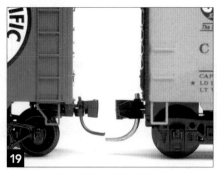

19

The N scale boxcar at left features a Z scale coupler, which is closer to scale dimensions than its N scale counterpart at right. Modeler Lance Mindheim made the modification. *Jim Forbe*

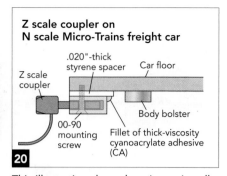

20

This illustration shows how Lance installs Z scale couplers on N scale Micro-Trains freight cars. *Rick Johnson*

21

Body-mounted couplers are the standard on HO scale locomotives and freight cars (left). Train set models and older models feature truck-mounted couplers (right).

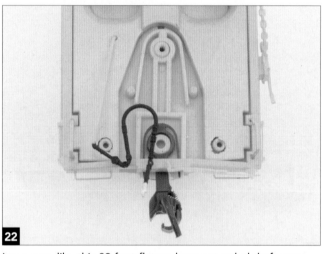

22

Long cars, like this 89-foot flatcar, have extended draft-gear boxes to negotiate tight curves on model railroads. These HO cars look their best operating on 24" or broader curves.

which are also available as separate items, feature coil metal knuckle springs, phosphor bronze centering springs, and metal trip pins.

Locomotives produced by MTH Electric Trains feature remote-control couplers that are compatible with the company's proprietary Digital Command System or Digital Command Control, **10**. These couplers are oversized, so it slightly increases the distance over the coupler pulling faces. MTH includes non-remote-controlled couplers for modelers who don't want that feature.

Although the couplers offered by various manufacturers look prototypical, they're actually oversized a bit to operate more reliably. It wasn't until the late 1990s and early 2000s that companies like Accurail, Kadee, McHenry (Athearn), and

Sergent Engineering began offering scale couplers, **11**. Not only are these couplers smaller in size, but they bring the distance between cars to a more prototypical distance.

Kadee and McHenry also produce lower-shelf and double-shelf couplers to match those found on prototype locomotives and freight cars, **12**. Kadee's couplers follow the Type F design; McHenry's are based on the Type E design.

N scale couplers

In the half century that N scale has been around, there has been a great deal of change in couplers. Rapido, an early manufacturer of N scale models (not to be confused with today's Rapido Trains), let other companies use its coupler design, **13**. The wedge-front coupler, which was used on most

N scale models (except Micro-Trains) through the 1990s, pivoted up and down. This allowed one coupler to ride over the other for coupling. Although the Rapido did a good job of keeping cars coupled, it—like the horn-hook in HO—was oversized and didn't look like a prototype knuckle coupler.

While coupling with Rapido couplers was easy, uncoupling cars was often difficult. Most modelers would lift one car off the rails. This proved tricky because the car would then have to be put back on the rails. Often times uncoupling in this manner would cause adjacent cars to derail.

Uncoupling ramps for Rapido couplers afforded some degree of automatic uncoupling. However, the ramps were fussy to deal with and required precise car placement to work properly. It also relied on the couplers

23

Like most contemporary N scale locomotives and freight cars, this BLMA covered hopper has body-mounted couplers. Body mounting is generally preferable for both appearance and operation.

24

These clear Aztec test cars show how truck-mounted couplers (top) put skewing force on the trucks when cars are pushed. With body-mounted couplers (bottom), the force is transmitted to the car body, which pulls the trucks along. *Jim Forbes*

25

The couplers on some Athearn models are secured in the draft-gear box with metal covers that snap in place. Hard coupling may cause the metal cover to pop off.

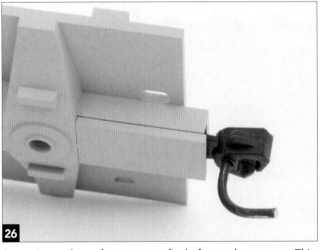

26

Some Accurail cars feature press-fit draft-gear box covers. This style of cover could work loose over time. Securing the covers with glue made maintenance difficult.

making contact with the uncoupling ramp, potentially causing a derailment.

The Magne-Matic era

Following on the success of its HO scale knuckle coupler, Kadee introduced an N scale version of its Magne-Matic operating knuckle coupler in the late 1960s. The spring-loaded coupler is split in half vertically. The knuckle is on the top half of the shank, while the rest of the coupler head is on the bottom half, **14**. The coupler opens and closes in a scissors action.

In 1990, Kadee split into two companies, Kadee (HO and larger scales) and Micro-Trains (N and Z scales).

For many years, the only way you could get factory-installed Magne-Matic couplers was by purchasing a Micro-Trains freight car. In recent years, other companies have been offering models with Micro-Trains couplers, including BLMA Models, Eastern Seaboard Models, Fox Valley Models, and Trainworx.

Today, Micro-Trains produces coupler conversion kits for many current and former N scale locomotives and freight cars. The company also offers a variety of truck-mounted couplers, as well as assembled couplers and coupler kits designed for body mounting. You can familiarize yourself with Magne-Matic couplers by

purchasing the N scale coupler starter set, item no. 1059, **15**.

New coupler manufacturers

Similar to HO scale, the late 1990s saw a growth in N scale automatic couplers from other manufacturers. Accurail (Accumate, found on Atlas models), Bachmann (E-Z Mate), and McHenry (Athearn) all offer plastic knuckle couplers, **16**. The couplers all follow the designs of their HO scale counterparts. Kato uses a proprietary line of couplers on its locomotives and rolling stock, **17**.

All of these brands perform well while coupling, but you may find occasional cross-compatibility issues when uncoupling.

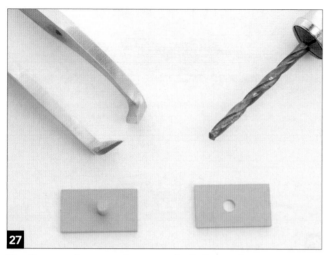

27 The first step in converting press-fit draft-gear box covers to screw-mount is to cut off the pin. Next, drill a screw clearance hole in the cover with a no. 43 bit.

28 Once the draft-gear boxes are installed, the trucks can be screwed in place.

29 Screw-mounted draft-gear box covers are the norm in HO scale. This is a Fox Valley Models boxcar.

30 Micro-Trains N scale cars feature mounting holes in the underframe for converting cars to body-mounted couplers.

Solid and other couplers

Solid-knuckle (non-automatic) couplers are offered by Con-Cor and InterMountain, **18**. These are handy for passenger trains, unit trains, and multiple-unit locomotive sets that don't require frequent uncoupling. They are pretty realistic, and also make close coupling on diesels possible. Uncoupling requires lifting an end of the car off the rails. Since solid-knuckle couplers aren't automatic, they're not prone to accidental uncoupling.

N scale lacks the scale-size and specialty couplers found in HO scale. However, some N scale modelers use Z scale couplers. Lance Mindheim installed Z scale couplers on his N scale cars to give them are more scale appearance, **19**. All that's required

is assembled Z scale couplers, .020" styrene, a drill and tap set for 00-90 screws, and thick cyanoacrylate adhesive, **20**. You can learn more about this technique in the January 2007 issue of *Model Railroader*.

Truck- vs. body-mounted couplers

Prototype locomotives and freight cars have body-mounted couplers, but that hasn't always been the case on HO and N scale models. Most contemporary HO locomotives and freight cars have body-mounted couplers. Older models, especially those designed for train sets, used truck-mounted couplers, **21**.

Longer cars, such as passenger cars and 89-foot piggyback flatcars and auto racks, typically have extended

draft-gear boxes, **22**. This makes it possible for the cars to negotiate the sharp curves on model railroads. However, these longer cars look better operating on broader-radius curves (24" or larger in HO).

In N scale, truck-mounted couplers were the standard for many years. Today, almost all locomotives and most newly tooled freight cars have body-mounted couplers, **23**. The primary reasons for making the switch from truck-mounted couplers to body-mounted couplers are a more prototypical appearance and better operation.

While the appearance between truck- and body-mounted couplers isn't that obvious at casual glance, the difference between the two quickly becomes apparent during switching

31 You can convert truck-mounted couplers to body-mounted. Use a no. 17 blade or jeweler's saw to remove the draft-gear boxes, then preserve the coupler and box for use on the car.

32 Once the draft-gear boxes have been removed, use a no. 60 bit to enlarge the hole to accept a 00-90 screw. The no. 60 bit can also be used to clear the hole in the underframe.

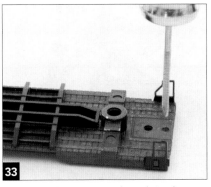

33 Use a 00-90 tap to cut threads in the hole drilled in the car floor. If the floor is metal, add a drop of oil to the tap to prevent it from sticking. Work slowly.

34 This Trainworx four-bay hopper features a base with a factory-drilled hole for attaching the draft-gear box. Smooth the ejector-pin mark to ensure the box seats properly.

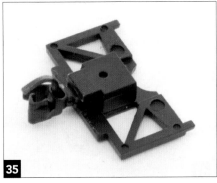

35 Trainworx offers two different N scale body-mount magnetic coupler conversions, including this one for the Atlas 90-ton hopper. Tutorial videos on the company's website, www.train-worx.com, show how to adapt the conversions for other models.

operations. When cars with truck-mounted couplers are shoved in reverse on curves, the force on the couplers causes the trucks to rotate outward, which can lead to derailments.

With body-mounted couplers, the force is transferred through the bodies, which pull the trucks along. This eliminates the turning force and lessens the chance for derailments, **24**.

HO scale installation
Some modelers prefer using one brand of coupler, while others keep whatever brand came with the model. So what do you do if you want to replace couplers? In HO scale, start by removing the draft-gear (coupler) box covers. Depending on the manufacturer, the covers may be secured with a metal clip, press-fit pin, or a small screw.

Metal clips are used on older Athearn models, **25**. The clips are held

in place by two plastic tabs. These tabs are delicate, and a hard coupling can cause plates to pop off and the couplers to fall out of the draft-gear box. If this becomes a problem on a specific car, you can cut off the existing draft-gear box and add a new one under the car floor, being careful to shim it to the proper height.

Some manufacturers prefer using press-fit draft-gear box covers, **26**. However, press-fit covers may work loose over time. Gluing the covers in place will work, but it makes it difficult if coupler maintenance and replacement is necessary.

Press-fit covers can usually be easily converted to screw-mounted. First, cut off the press-fit pin. Then drill a no. 43 clearance hole in the draft-gear box cover, **27**.

Next, check the mounting hole with a no. 50 bit. If the hole is smaller, open

it up with the bit. If it's larger, fill the hole with styrene, then drill a new hole with a no. 50 bit. Once the holes are complete, thread them with a 2-56 tap and use a 2-56 screw to mount it, **28**.

Factory screw-mounted draft-gear box covers have become the standard in HO, **29**. These make it easy to replace couplers and perform maintenance.

N scale installation
Even though more N scale models are being offered with body-mounted couplers, there are still scores of cars out there with truck-mounted couplers. The ease of converting these cars to body-mounted couplers varies among manufacturers.

Micro-Trains cars with truck-mounted couplers have mounting holes in the underframe for body mounting, **30**. Start by removing the draft-gear boxes with a no. 17 chisel blade or a

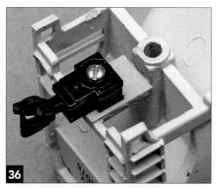

36

You can make body-mount conversions for N scale cars using styrene strip. Former *Model Railroader* managing editor Jim Kelly did just that on this 1990s-era Atlas hopper. *Jim Kelly*

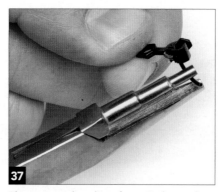

37

These specialty pliers from Kadee make it easy to fix low-hanging trip pins. Micro-Trains offers a similar tool for N scale couplers. *Jim Forbes*

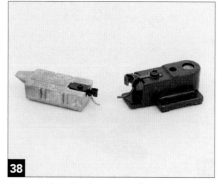

38

Gauges for checking coupler and trip pin height are offered in HO scale by Kadee (right) and Micro-Mark. The N scale gauge (left) is from Micro-Trains Line.

39

A low coupler is problematic, as it may cause cars to uncouple or the trip pin to snag on turnouts or crossings. The pin on this coupler is at the correct height per the Micro-Mark HO scale coupler height gauge (no. 82824). *Jim Forbes*

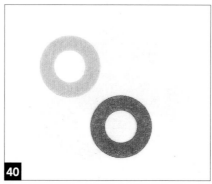

40

Kadee fiber washers are good for making small coupler height adjustments. They're offered in .010" (gray) and .015" (red) thicknesses, and are placed between the truck and car bolster. *Jim Forbes*

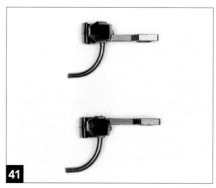

41

If the difference in coupler height is more than a fiber washer or styrene shim can fix, try using underset- or overset-shank couplers. Both styles of couplers are available in HO and N scales.

jeweler's saw, **31**. Then use a no. 60 bit to enlarge the hole in the draft-gear boxes to clear a 00-90 screw, **32**. Also use the bit to clear the holes in the underframe.

With the draft-gear boxes prepared, use a tap to make threads in the car floor, **33**. If the floor is metal, apply a drop of light oil to the tap so it doesn't stick. Regardless of the material, work slowly and back the tap out periodically to remove any plastic or metal shavings.

Other manufacturers have holes or dimples for body-mounting draft-gear boxes, **34**. Use the same steps for the Micro-Trains cars on these models.

Body-mounting couplers on cars without locating holes or cars without mounting platforms is a bit trickier. However, there are products that make this easier. Trainworx Inc. offers the factory-assembled nos. 620 and

622 body-mount magnetic coupler conversions, **35**. The 620 is designed for Precision Masters and Red Caboose Ortner five-bay rapid-discharge hoppers. The 622 is for the Atlas 90-ton three-bay hopper.

With modification the conversions can be adapted for other models. Trainworx has videos on how to make these modifications on its website, www.train-worx.com.

You can also make your own body-mount conversion. Jim Kelly, former *Model Railroader* managing editor and longtime N scale modeler, used styrene strip to build a mounting platform for a 1990s-era Atlas covered hopper, **36**.

Testing and maintenance

In both HO and N scales, it's important that couplers are mounted at the proper height. Couplers at

mismatched heights are prone to uncoupling. Low-hanging trip pins are also problematic, as they can snag on turnouts and grade crossings, causing derailments and damage to equipment. Trip pins can be adjusted using special pliers offered by Kadee and Micro-Trains, **37**.

However, bending the trip pin too high can impact how it actuates. The trip pin should be 1⁄32" above the railhead in HO scale, and .010" in N.

Kadee and Micro-Trains offer coupler height gauges in HO and N scale, respectively, **38**. Before any locomotive or freight car is used on a model railroad, the couplers should be checked against the gauge. The top of the couplers on the model should be at the same height as the top of the coupler on the gauge. The trip pin should clear the small shelf on the HO gauge or the metal plate supplied with the N scale gauge. This ensures that the pin is appropriately spaced above the railhead and won't snag on turnout rails or grade crossings.

A word of caution regarding coupler height gauges. The Kadee no. 205 and Micro-Trains no. 1055 gauges are metal. If placed on a model railroad when the power is turned on, the gauge will cause a short circuit. Kadee offers the no. 206 gauge, which is safe to use on live track.

The most common problem you'll encounter with couplers is that they're too low, **39**. There are a few fixes for this. In HO scale, the first is to add a Kadee fiber washer, **40**, to the bolster before screwing the truck in place. This raises the end of the car, thus raising the coupler. Kadee washers are offered in two thicknesses: .010" (gray) and .015" (red). Washers are fine for small adjustments, but only use one washer. Multiple washers may fix the coupler height, but they'll raise the car to an unrealistic height. Multiple washers may also cause the car to rock side to side when in motion.

In rare instances, the coupler may be too high. To fix this on cars with separate draft-gear boxes, you can insert a thin piece of styrene (.005", .010", or .015") as a shim above the draft-gear box.

A good solution for either high or low couplers is to use an overset- or underset-shank coupler. These are offered in N and HO scales, **41**.

Uncoupling options
Uncoupling can be done automatically with permanent magnets or electromagnets. In HO scale, Kadee sells delayed and non-delayed uncoupling permanent magnets that fit between the rails, as well as under-the-track and electric delayed-uncoupling magnets. The permanent magnets are polarized across the rails. An electromagnet only works when a button is pushed to activate it.

In N scale, Micro-Trains offers two styles of magnets. The under-the-ties no. 308 is easy to hide with ballast or other scenery material. If you're okay with the magnet being visible, the

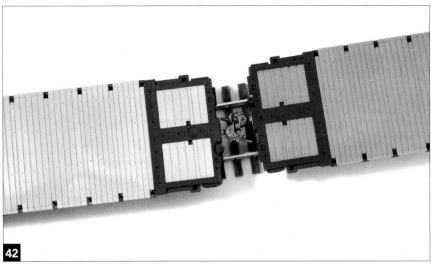
42

Delayed uncoupling is a multi-step process. It allows a car to be uncoupled and then shoved to its final spot. *Bill Zuback*

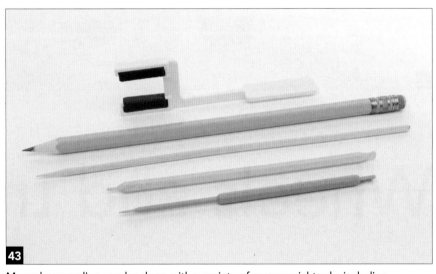
43

Manual uncoupling can be done with a variety of commercial tools, including the Accumate Switchman, Kadee Dual Tool, and Rix Sticker. Common household products, like a pencil or bamboo skewer, may also be used.

no. 1310 (magnet only) and no. 1311 (magnet secured in a 5" section of Atlas track) are options.

How does delayed uncoupling work? First, stop the cars over an uncoupling magnet. As soon as there's slack in the coupling, the metal trip pins will pull the knuckles apart. Next, pull the train forward slightly until the couplers are spread in the delay position.

Then carefully push back to the uncoupled car. The couplers will engage but not couple, **42**. Push the car to the desired location, then back away and the couplers will return to their normal position.

Automatic uncoupling is best reserved for sidings and secondary

lines where setouts and pickups are made. Experienced modelers rarely put magnets on the main line, as accidental uncoupling can occur. If you want to put a magnet on the main, consider using an electromagnet.

Some modelers find the forward-and-back move to set the couplers in the delay position unnecessary and non-prototypical. If you don't want to use magnets on your layout, try manual uncoupling. This can be done using an assortment of commercially made uncoupling tools, such as the Accumate Switchman, Kadee Dual Tool, and Rix Sticker, among others, **43**. Other modelers prefer simpler tools, such as a bamboo skewer or pencil.

1

CHAPTER EIGHT

Wheels and trucks

In railroading, a truck is the entire rolling assembly including sideframes, wheels, axles, springs, and brake gear. Most freight car trucks have two axles (four wheels). This is a double-truss, solid-bearing truck dating from the late steam/early diesel era.

Wheels and trucks are important components of a smooth-running freight car, **1**. In this chapter, we'll take an up-close look at some of the prototype wheels and trucks used over the years, explore the different versions available in HO and N scales, and provide tips on installing and maintaining trucks and wheelsets on your freight cars.

2

Cast-iron ("chilled") wheels, were common on early freight cars, and can be spotted by their ribbed backs. They were banned from interchange after 1970.

3

Cast or wrought steel wheels have been in use since the 1920s, and have been used on all new freight cars since 1958. Steel wheels have plain (non-ribbed) backs. These feature roller bearings on the axle ends.

4

This Railbox boxcar is equipped with 33"-diameter wheels. This size of wheel is used on rolling stock with a capacity of 70 tons and less.

5

Freight cars with 100-ton capacity, such as this TrinityRail 5,161-cubic-foot-capacity covered hopper, are fitted with 36"-diameter wheels.

Prototype wheels

Wheels on prototype freight cars have changed over the years. Cast-iron wheels (also called "chilled" wheels for the heat-treating process used on them) were common on early freight cars, **2**. They usually had ribs on the back, which helped dissipate heat created by braking. These wheels were not allowed on new or newly rebuilt cars as of Jan. 1, 1958; they couldn't be interchanged after 1970.

Cast and wrought steel wheels (without ribbed backs) started appearing in the 1920s, **3**. As the steam era wound down, steel wheels were the norm on most freight cars. Today's freight cars all have wheels of wrought or cast steel.

Much like tires on a car, steel freight car wheels have a lifespan. Single-wear

wheels (1W) have 1¼" rims and are scrapped after the tread wears down. Two-wear wheels (2W), which have 2" rims, can be turned to remove flat spots (these are what make the "ka-chunk, ka-chunk" sound you occasionally hear as a freight car rolls by) and restore them to their proper contour. The wheel style (1W or 2W) and size are often indicated on the car ends. This ensures the proper wheels are installed when repairs are made to the car.

A common question asked by new modelers is, "What size wheels should I use on my freight cars?" The answer depends on the car's capacity. Cars with a capacity of 70 tons or less (and most cabooses) use 33"-diameter wheels, **4**. Covered hoppers, tank cars, gondolas, and other cars with a capacity of 100 tons have 36"-diameter wheels, **5**. The

intermediate wheels on articulated 125-ton capacity well cars feature 38"-diameter wheels (the end trucks have 33"-diameter wheels), **6**. A caveat to this rule is modern tri-level auto racks. The wheels on these cars are 28" diameter to keep the car profile low for clearance purposes.

Prototype trucks

A variety of truck designs have been used by railroads since the early 1900s. There isn't space to show the hundreds of variations here. Instead, we'll focus on the common designs used on prototype cars (and commonly found on models).

In **7** you can see the basic components of a freight car truck. The freight car bolster and and kingpin rest in the truck's center plate.

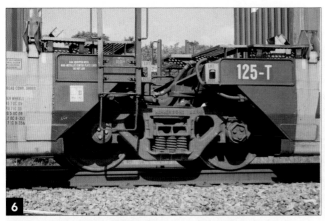

6

The 125-ton intermediate trucks on this articulated well car have 38"-diameter wheels (left). The end trucks on the A and B units have 33"-diameter wheels.

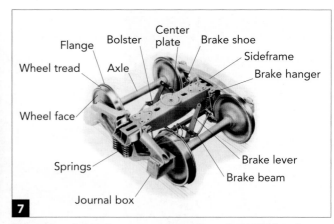

7

This image shows the components of a typical solid-bearing freight car truck. *Buckeye Steel Castings Co.*

8

Cotton waste soaked with lubricating oil is stuffed in journal boxes on solid-bearing trucks (visible with the box cover open). The oil keeps the axle end and bearing lubricated.

9

Archbar trucks were commonly used on freight cars into the early 1900s. The pressed steel parts were bolted together, giving them a distinctive appearance. *Jeff Wilson*

The truck bolster isn't anchored to the two sideframes. Instead, it sits on top of a spring package in each sideframe. The truck's capacity determines the number of springs and their size. For example, a 50-ton truck has fewer and smaller springs than a 100-ton truck. The springs help the bolster float in the sideframes, helping cars ride down the rails smoothly.

Trucks are rated by the total weight (car and load) they can carry. That means a 70-ton truck can be used on a car that has a 70-ton load capacity.

The weight of the sideframes is carried by the axle ends. Older cars featured solid-bearing (often incorrectly called friction-bearing) trucks. On these trucks, the axle ends and bearings were enclosed in a journal box. The boxes were packed with waste, a cotton-fiber material soaked with lubricating oil, **8**. The oil would wick from the waste and lubricate the bearings and axle ends.

Archbar and Andrews trucks

There were many types of solid-bearing trucks used on freight cars in the first half of the 20th century. Archbar trucks were common into the early 1900s, **9**. These pressed-steel trucks featured parts that were bolted together. Though reliable, the trucks needed frequent regular maintenance to tighten bolts that worked loose. The archbar design lasted into the 1920s. Cars equipped with archbar trucks couldn't be interchanged after 1941.

Cast sideframes remedied the maintenance issues that plagued archbar trucks. An early popular style was the Andrews, **10**. Andrews trucks had separate journal boxes secured with bolts (boxes from archbar trucks could be installed on Andrews trucks, which was a key selling point). An identifying feature of the Andrews truck is a steel bar between the bottom of the journal box and the sideframe. Andrews trucks were in production from 1910 through

the 1930s. They were banned from interchange after 1956.

Bettendorf and ARA trucks

Journal boxes that were cast integral with the sideframe was the next step in truck evolution. The first manufacturer to do this was the Bettendorf Co. Its T-section truck, **11**, had diamond-shaped sideframes. The truck, which had chords with a T-shaped cross section, was introduced in the early 1900s and was popular through the 1910s.

Trucks with U-shaped sideframe cross sections replaced the T-section trucks, **12**. The U-section designs, common throughout the late steam and beginning of the diesel era, were stronger than their predecessors with a wider cross section. The American Railway Association (ARA, later the American Association of Railroads, AAR) adopted the U-section cast steel trucks as its Type Y standard truck.

10

This is an Andrews truck. The cast-metal sideframes featured separate journal boxes that were bolted in place. A snubber is used in place of one of the springs.

11

The Bettendorf T-section truck featured journal boxes cast into the sideframe. The diamond-shaped sideframes and T cross section are hallmarks of this truck. *Trains magazine collection*

12

The U-section truck was adopted as the American Railway Association Type Y standard truck, with several manufacturers building versions. This truck was built by American Steel Foundries for the Northern Pacific Ry.

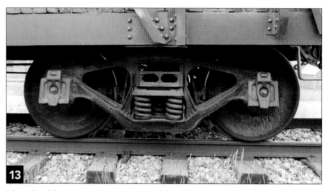

13

The double-truss design resembles the U-section truck, but with the open leg of the U filled in for additional strength. Solid-bearing trucks of this design were used on freight cars into the 1980s.

The U-shaped cross-section truck has incorrectly become known as a Bettendorf truck. While the Bettendorf Co. did license parts of the truck's design, other manufacturers produced trucks of this style. This led to variations in the size and type of springs, sideframe outline, journal-box lids, and bolster design.

While the ARA adopted the U-section truck as standard, companies looked to improve on the design. In the 1930s, the double-truss sideframe enhanced the AAR standard, **13**. At first glance, the double-truss truck looks like other trucks from the period. However, upon closer examination, you'll see that portions of the U-shaped cross section are filled in.

Enhancing the standard

When it had been established that double-truss trucks and U-section cast-steel sideframes were proven strong enough to do the job, the next period of truck development was improving

how they rode. The big goals were to cut down the amount of vertical and lateral movement. Too much movement wears out wheels and springs prematurely, takes a toll on track and roadbed, and can lead to damaged lading and derailments.

The Dalman design was an early effort to improve the riding characteristics of trucks, **14**. The distinctive truck, which dates back to the 1920s, had eight springs per sideframe (five were typical on most trucks) at different levels and sported a unique sideframe design.

The World War II era saw the arrival of what would become the two most popular trucks through the 1960s: the Barber S-2, **15**, and the American Steel Foundries (ASF) A-3 Ride Control, **16**. The Barber S-2 truck was common from the late steam through the early diesel era, and the ASF A-3 quickly grew in popularity. From the end of the war through the conclusion of the solid-bearing era, the A-3 truck

was the most popular. While the two trucks are similar in appearance, there are spotting differences around the spring packages and bolster ends.

The National B-1 was one of many stabilized trucks introduced to improve ride quality, **17**. The two circles at the bottom of the sideframe and the spring package with stabilizing wedges make the B-1 easy to distinguish from other styles of trucks.

A variety of manufacturers produced freight car trucks during the steam era and through the 1960s. Among them were American Steel Foundries (ASF), Bettendorf Co., Buckeye, National, and Standard Car Truck Co. A quick way to identify trucks is to read the information cast into the sideframe. Typical sideframe data includes the manufacturer name, truck type, spring package type, and occasionally the name of the railroad.

The knock on solid-bearing trucks was the amount of labor required to maintain them. Frequent lubrication

14

The Dalman truck stood out amongst its contemporaries because it had eight springs (on different levels) instead of the typical five. *Trains magazine collection*

15

The Barber S-2 was a common solid-bearing truck of the late steam and early diesel era. This one was built for the Chicago, Burlington & Quincy.

16

Another product from the World War II era was the American Steel Foundries A-3 Ride Control truck. This was the most popular truck from the end of the war until the end of the solid-bearing era.

17

The National B-1 is a stabilized truck that first appeared in the early 1930s. Two circles at the bottom of the sideframe and stabilizing wedges in the spring package make the truck easy to identify. *Northern Pacific*

was a must, otherwise the bearing would become dry, resulting in a journal-box fire (hence the term "hot box") or a broken axle. Solid-bearing trucks were no longer used on new cars built after 1966; they were banned from interchange in the 1990s.

Roller-bearing trucks

Though we think of roller-bearing trucks in terms of newer cars, they date back to the turn of the 20th century. In the 1930s, roller-bearing trucks were used on passenger cars. However, they were cost-prohibitive to use in large numbers on freight equipment. That started to change in the 1950s and 1960s, when roller-bearing trucks came into widespread use.

Some solid-bearing trucks were converted to roller-bearing trucks, **18**.

Roller-bearing trucks can easily be identified by looking at the end caps on the axle ends, which rotate

when the car is in motion. The two leading roller-bearing trucks are the Barber S-2, **19**, and the ASF Ride Control, **20**. The trucks are produced by Standard Car Truck Co. and ASF-Keystone, respectively. If these trucks and manufacturers sound familiar, they should, as both produced trucks during the solid-bearing era.

Other modern trucks not shown here are the National C-1 and ASF Ridemaster. All modern trucks are offered in versions between 70 and 125 tons with an assortment of spring packages.

Caboose trucks

To help provide a smooth ride for crew members, cabooses were equipped with trucks that featured different springing than their freight car counterparts. A typical caboose weighs about half of what a similarly sized freight car does, so elliptical leaf springs could be used

in place of coil springs. As with freight car trucks, there were many variations. A few examples include the Barber S-2 with solid bearings, **21**, and the Barber-Bettendorf with roller bearings, **22**. Some railroads, such as the Milwaukee Road, used GSC trucks based on passenger-car designs, **23**.

HO and N scale wheels

The greatest variety of wheelsets is found in HO scale. One-piece plastic castings and plastic or metal wheels on a separate axle (plastic, brass, or steel) are among the options available.

The stock wheels on many HO models have a .110" wheel tread width (flange and tread), which is compatible with most model track. This is also the width noted in National Model Railroad Association (NMRA) Recommended Practice 25. However, these wheels are significantly wider than those found on prototype cars.

18 Many solid-bearing trucks were converted to roller bearings. They're easy to spot, as the journal-box covers are removed for the conversion.

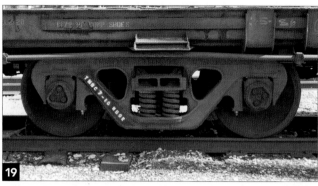

19 This Barber S-2 70-ton roller-bearing truck is on an 89-foot piggyback flatcar. 70-ton trucks have two visible springs; 100-ton trucks have three.

20 The ASF Ride Control truck is offered in 70- through 125-ton versions. Originally built for the Soo Line, this 100-ton truck is on a Minnesota Northern Pullman-Standard 4,427-cubic-foot-capacity covered hopper.

21 If you compare this Barber S-2 caboose truck to the freight car version in photo 15, you can see they follow similar lines. The big difference is the elliptical leaf springs used on this truck, which provides a smoother ride for the crew.

To address the oversized .110" wheels, some manufacturers have produced "semi-scale" wheels with a tread width of .088". Though narrower, the wheels still operate on most commercial track. There are instances where .088" wheels may fall into flangeways on some turnouts. It's always best to run a test car with semi-scale wheels across your layout to check for trouble spots before replacing the wheelsets on all your freight cars.

A few manufacturers offer wheels that are truly scale size, following specific prototype dimensions. These wheels are used by modelers building their layout to fine scale, or Proto:87, standards. For a comparison of the three wheel styles, see **24**.

Scale wheels look terrific, but they unfortunately aren't compatible with most commercial track. Sectional turnouts and crossings are designed with wider tolerances, which means scale wheels can drop into flangeways and turnout frog gaps.

For many years, Micro-Trains N scale cars featured one-piece plastic wheelsets with oversized flanges, dubbed "pizza cutters" by modelers. While the wheelsets worked well on code 80 track (track with rails .080" tall), they proved problematic on code 55 (.055"-tall) rail, which has gained in popularity for its near-scale appearance. The oversized flanges bump the molded spike heads on the track.

Micro-Trains now offers wheelsets with shallow flanges, which perform well on code 55 track. You can see the differences in flanges in **25**.

In addition, a variety of manufacturers produce metal wheelsets in various prototypical diameters, including BLMA (now Atlas Model Railroad Co.), Con-Cor, Fox Valley Models, InterMountain, and NorthWest Short Line, among others.

Regardless of the scale, if you replace stock wheelsets with after-market offerings, make sure the new wheelsets will fit in the trucks. Most replacement wheelsets specify the axle length or the specific trucks for which the wheelsets are designed.

Plastic or metal wheelsets?

One debate among modelers is whether to use plastic or metal wheels. The discussion has quieted down in HO scale circles, as most new models come with metal wheelsets. However, in N scale there are still a sizeable number of models with plastic wheelsets.

On the surface, the choice may seem obvious. Real trains use metal wheels, so our models should too, right? However, plastic does have some advantages. If the wheels and axle are a single casting, such as those found on Accurail (HO) and Micro-Trains (N) freight cars, the wheels will stay in gauge, **26**. That doesn't hold true on wheelsets included with Athearn and Model Die Casting (Roundhouse) HO kits, where the plastic wheels were mounted on a metal axle, **27**.

22

The most popular caboose truck of the roller-bearing era was the Barber-Bettendorf. This truck features swing-motion elliptical leaf springs.

23

Milwaukee Road's ribbed-side bay-window cabooses rode on trucks built at the railroad's shops. Other railroads used similar trucks based on passenger-car designs.

24

Compare the three tread widths on these HO 33"-diameter metal wheelsets. From top is a .110" tread from Kadee, a semi-scale .088" tread from InterMountain, and a scale-width tread from NorthWest Short Line. *Jeff Wilson*

25

The flanges on Micro-Trains' original N scale wheelsets (left) were oversized, earning them the nickname "pizza cutters." Today's Micro-Trains cars have shallow-flange wheels (right) that look better and roll well on code 55 rail.

26

Accurail (HO, right) and Micro-Trains (N, left) wheelsets are one-piece plastic castings. Unless the axle is damaged, the wheels will stay in gauge.

27

Plastic wheelsets are non-conductive and develop a static charge. This tends to accumulate a buildup of dirt and grime on the wheel treads.

28

For realistic appearance, paint the front and back of each wheel and the axle. Keep paint off the wheel treads and the tip of the needlepoint axle. *Bill Zuback*

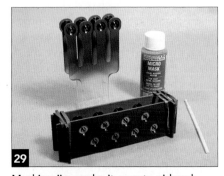

29

Masking jigs make it easy to airbrush several wheelsets at once. The axle tips should be masked with a product like Microscale Micro Mask. *Andy Sperandeo*

Plastic also has the benefit of being non-magnetic. This matters if you use magnetic uncoupling ramps. Some wheelsets use steel axles, which are magnetic and can be pulled toward the magnet, potentially causing an unwanted uncoupling.

While plastic wheelsets have some advantages, they also have drawbacks. The major challenge is the amount of dirt that plastic wheel treads accumulate. Since plastic wheels are non-conductive, they develop a static charge. This attracts dirt, dust, and other debris that builds up on the tread, **27**.

Metal wheelsets have a variety of advantages. First, the friction of the metal wheels on metal rails helps polish both surfaces. Metal wheelsets also add extra weight to models and help lower their center of gravity.

The shiny tread on metal wheels is also nice, but the wheel face and back should have a rusty-brown appearance. Whether it's a chemically blackened or shiny metal, you can give metal wheelsets a realistic appearance using a multi-step process. First, wipe the entire wheel with a cotton swab soaked

30

Most new freight car trucks, such as these HO scale American Car & Foundry Archbars from Tahoe Model Works, have sideframes of acetal or other slippery engineering plastic. Plastic molding enables re-creation of fine details. *Jim Forbes*

31

Kadee produces a variety of die-cast metal trucks in HO scale. The trucks have metal springs that the bolster floats on, similar to a prototype truck. *Jim Forbes*

32

Micro-Trains N scale cars use a friction pin to secure the truck to the bolster on the car's underbody.

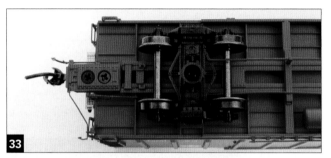

33

The trucks on this ExactRail HO boxcar are secured with screws. Note the metal wheelsets and brake-beam detail.

Wheel and truck manufacturers

The following is a directory of companies that produce freight car trucks and/or wheelsets in HO and/or N scales

Accurail
www.accurail.com

Athearn
www.athearn.com

Atlas Model Railroad Co.
www.atlasrr.com

Bachmann
www.bachmanntrains.com

BLMA
www.atlasrr.com

Bowser
www.bowser-trains.com

Con-Cor
www.con-cor.com

Eastern Car Works
No website

Fox Valley Models
www.foxvalleymodels.com

InterMountain
www.intermountain-railway.com

Jay-Bee
www.jbwheelsets.com

Kadee
www.kadee.com

Kato
www.katousa.com

Model Die Casting (Roundhouse)
www.athearn.com

Micro-Trains
www.micro-trains.com

NorthWest Short Line
www.nwsl.com

Precision Scale Co.
www.precisionscaleco.com

Rapido Trains
www.rapidotrains.com

Reboxx
www.reboxx.com

Ring Engineering
www.ringengineering.com

Tahoe Model Works
resincarworks.com/tahoe.htm

Tangent Scale Models
www.tangentscalemodels.com

Tichy Train Group
www.tichytraingroup.com

Wm. K. Walthers
www.walthers.com

in 70 percent isopropyl alcohol. This will remove oil and other residue from the manufacturing process that may affect paint adhesion.

Next, apply a flat, dark-brown paint (Railroad Tie Brown, Dark Rust, and Roof Brown are a few of my favorites) to the front and back of the wheel and the axle, **28**. Keep paint off the tread and tip of the axle. If you're painting wheelsets for a few cars, a Microbrush is a quick option. If you're painting a large quantity of wheelsets and have an airbrush, consider using a wheel masking jig such as those from American Model Builders, Modeler's Choice (both shown in **29**), and MinuteMan Scale models. The tips of

34 Replacing a snap-fit truck requires a bit of work. After filling the hole with putty or styrene rod, drill and tap the bolster for a new screw and secure the truck.

35 Painting the molded springs and roller-bearing adapters (just above the axle end caps) in contrasting colors adds to the realism of truck sideframes. *Bill Zuback*

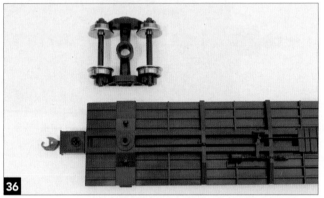
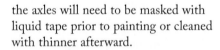

36 Check the truck bolster and truck sideframes for flash. The excess plastic that oozes out of a mold can cause a car to lean, rock, or wobble, potentially causing a derailment.

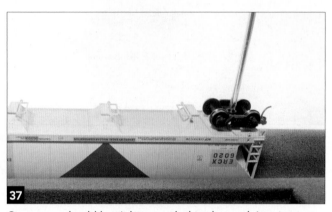

37 One screw should be tight enough that the truck just rotates freely. The other screw should be loose enough that the truck has some lateral and longitudinal play.

the axles will need to be masked with liquid tape prior to painting or cleaned with thinner afterward.

Model trucks

The majority of today's HO scale trucks—and all N scale—are made of acetal or other engineering plastic that makes it possible to re-create fine detail, **30**. This plastic is also self-lubricating, which helps the needle-point axles roll freely.

Kadee and other manufacturers produce die-cast metal or brass trucks in HO scale, **31**. Kadee's trucks also feature metal springs which, like the prototype, the bolster floats on.

Trucks are secured to models either by snap fit, a friction pin, **32**, or a screw, **33**. Snap-fit trucks were once used on train-set and entry-level models, but aren't common today. Friction pins can be found on older Accurail HO scale kits and Micro-Trains N scale models.

The trucks on almost all HO scale (and an increasing number of N scale) models are held with screws.

Replacing trucks on a model isn't usually difficult. Just remove the screw or friction pin, replace the truck, and replace the friction pin or screw. If the model featured snap-fit trucks, a bit more work is required. Fill the mounting hole with a styrene tube glued in place or modeling putty. Then drill an appropriate-size hole and tap the hole for the proper screw, **34**.

Acetal trucks look nice, but hobby paint doesn't stick well to engineering plastic. It's not a necessity, but one option is to first spray them with two coats of Specialty Performance Products Plastic Adhesion Promoter no. SXA-1050 or Tamiya Color for Polycarbonate. Plastic Adhesion Promoter is designed for use by auto body repair professionals. Use it in a well-ventilated area, wear personal

protective gear, and follow all warning information printed on the label. The same goes for the Tamiya Color for Polycarbonate.

Ten minutes after the second coat of Plastic Adhesion Promoter is applied, the trucks are ready for weathering. To keep paint out of the sockets, install old wheelsets or mask the holes with tape or Silly Putty. Apply the paint with a brush, or with an airbrush in light coats.

Trucks can be further enhanced by painting the springs and roller bearing adapters a contrasting color, **35**. When in doubt on how to weather trucks, use prototype photos as a guide.

Improving performance

When trucks and wheelsets are installed, the car should roll freely without wobbling. If the car leans to one side, wobbles, or rocks, check the bolster and center plate. These surfaces

38

Micro-Mark's Truck Tuner reams the sockets on plastic trucks so wheelsets can roll freely. *Jim Forbes*

39

To more accurately match the prototype's truck centers, and to provide more clearance between the trucks and corner steps, Jim Six moved the body bolsters on this HO caboose ³⁄₁₆" closer to center. *Jim Six*

40

The National Model Railroad Association standards gauge is offered in HO (left), N (right), and other scales. One of its many uses is to make sure wheels are correctly gauged.

41

A motor tool with wire brush, run at low speed, can be used to clean and polish freight car wheel treads. Be sure to wear eye protection when doing this.

should be even and free of flash (excess plastic that oozes out of a mold during the manufacturing process), **36**.

Truck mounting screws are also critical to how a freight car performs. One screw should be tight enough that the truck rotates freely. The other screw should be loose enough that the truck has some lateral and longitudinal play, **37**. If the car continues to wobble, adjust the looser screw until the problem is alleviated.

If a car doesn't roll freely, make sure the needle-point axles aren't binding in the truck socket. This may be caused by molding flash or the wheel sockets being too shallow for the axle. To remedy this, use Micro-Mark's HO scale Truck Tuner, **38**, or the Reboxx

Exxact Socket. The tuner snaps into the truck similar to a wheelset and reams the sockets at the correct 60-degree angle. This allows the wheelset to roll freely.

In addition, make sure the truck can rotate freely through its range of motion. There are times where the draft-gear box, center sill, or details may impede the travel of the truck. In those situations, body modifications may have to be made, **39**. This usually isn't a problem for plastic cars.

Before installing new wheelsets, make sure the wheels are centered on the axle and that they're in gauge using a National Model Railroad Association standards gauge, **40**. The notches in the gauge indicate the correct depth

of a flange based on NMRA RP-25. If the flanges are too deep, they may hit the molded spike heads on ties, or "pick" the points of a turnout, causing a derailment.

Except for one-piece plastic castings, most wheelsets can be adjusted by grasping the wheels and twisting them slightly on the axle. Once the wheels are properly gauged, use a drop of cyanoacrylate adhesive to hold the wheels in place.

The treads on metal wheels can be cleaned with a motor tool and a wire brush, **41**. Run the motor tool on low speed and wear eye protection. It's also important to keep the brush moving, as excess heat may cause it plastic sideframes to melt.

1

CHAPTER NINE

Tools and adhesives

Building, maintaining, and repairing freight cars and rolling stock requires the proper tools and adhesives. It also requires knowing which adhesives to use with various materials.

You don't need a large toolbox to get started in the hobby. A good beginner's tool kit can be completed with about a dozen items, **1**. When purchasing tools, get the best your hobby budget will allow, particularly if it's an item you plan on using frequently. The old adage "you get what you pay for" is often the case with hobby tools. Poor-quality tools can fail when you need them most. High-quality tools that are used properly and looked after will serve you well for many years.

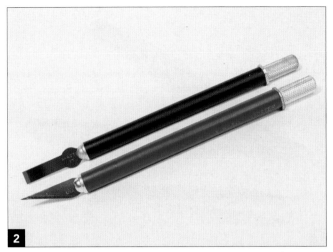

2 Hobby knives are essential for model building. The knife in the background has a chisel-tipped no. 17 blade. The knife in the foreground has a pointed-tip no. 11 blade.

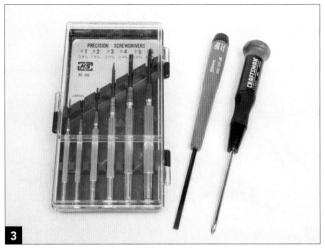

3 Various sizes of small straight (flat-blade) and Phillips-head screwdrivers make it easy to build models. You can purchase them in sets or individually.

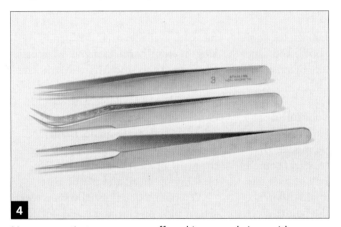

4 Non-magnetic tweezers are offered in several sizes with straight and curved tips. They make it easy to get into tights spots on a scale model (or hold small parts) that full-sized fingers can't reach.

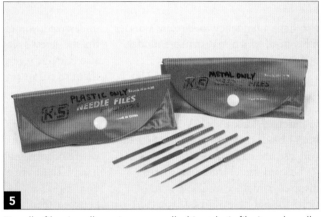

5 Needle files (small versions are called jeweler's files) work well for smoothing and cleaning up edges on plastic and metal parts. Metal lodged in the files may damage plastic, so it's a good idea to keep dedicated sets for each material.

Just as having the right tools for the job makes model railroading more enjoyable, so does using the correct adhesives. Though there are scenarios where more than one adhesive can be used on a project (such as cyanoacrylate adhesive and epoxy on resin models), adhesives are generally designed for a specific material like plastic or wood.

The tools and adhesives discussed here will get you started. As you gain experience, you're sure to add new items to your toolbox.

12 tools for beginners

Ask a group of hobbyists what tools you need to get started in model railroading and you'll probably get a variety of answers. Most modelers would probably agree with the first six items listed here. These are basic items that every model railroader will use. The second half dozen items would be considered useful additions to a beginner's toolbox.

It isn't necessary to dash to the hobby shop to buy all of these tools at once. Most modelers acquire tools on an as-needed basis. Start with the essentials and build up your tool inventory over time.

Hobby knife. A hobby knife with replaceable blades is an essential item for model building, **2**. Excel, Mascot Precision Tools, and X-acto are among the companies that offer handles and blades. The knives feature a metal or metal-and-plastic handle and a built-in chuck that holds the replaceable surgically sharp blade. Handle sizes include ¼", ½", and ¾" diameter. Since you'll probably use a hobby knife more than any other tool, select a handle that you can comfortably grip.

There are a variety of blades for hobby knives. The two most commonly used for model railroading are the pointed-tip no. 11 blade and the square-tip (chisel-tip) no. 17 blade. The no. 11 is good for most general work, such as cutting strip and sheet wood and styrene and trimming flash (excess plastic) from parts. The no. 17 is handy for removing molded details from models and cutting parts from sprues.

For best results, keep a sharp blade in your hobby knife. Dull blades don't cut as cleanly or quickly. Dull blades

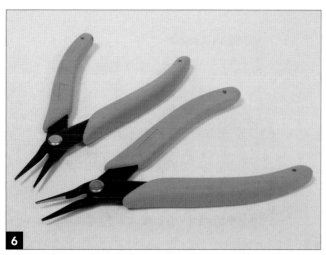

6

Among the uses for needlenose pliers are installing detail parts, bending wire, and holding small parts. They come in many sizes. The pliers shown here are from Xuron Corp., which makes a variety of pliers and cutting tools.

7

Sprue cutters are designed for removing plastic parts from molding sprues. The plier-style cutter (top) is a Mascot Precision Tools item. The tweezer-style stainless steel cutter, by Micro-Mark, leaves little plastic residue behind.

also have a tendency to slip and wander off course, which may damage models or cause injury.

Replacement blades are available in small refill packs, typically five per card. However, it's more economical to purchase bulk packs. A 100-pack of no. 11 blades sells for less than $40 and will last several months.

Discard used blades in a sharps disposal container, available at most well-stocked drug stores. If you can't find a sharps container, put used blades in a sealed plastic container, such as an empty juice bottle with a slot cut in the lid. Under no circumstances should you throw old blades directly into a garbage can.

Screwdrivers. If you're going to build or repair locomotives and freight cars, you'll need a set of miniature screwdrivers, **3**. Straight-blade and Phillips drivers are available in graduated sizes that will fit virtually any miniature screw.

Miniature screwdrivers are offered individually and in multi-piece sets (five or six) by Craftsman, General, Mascot, and Wiha, among others. Most sets are packed in a hard plastic case. To prevent screwdrivers from being misplaced, put them back in their case after each use.

Make sure the screwdriver you use is correctly sized for the job. If you use a screwdriver that's oversized or undersized, you may damage the tool's tip, the screw's slot, or both. You can also damage screwdrivers by misusing them to cut or pry.

Tweezers. Sometimes our full-size fingers are too big to handle and position parts on a scale model. That's where non-magnetic tweezers come in handy. There are a variety of tweezers on the market, **4**. The main difference between them lies in the points. Smooth points are ideal for handling delicate parts without marring the surface. For a more secure grip, use tweezers with serrated points. Whether smooth or serrated, tweezers should have sharp, fine points that are properly aligned.

The points on most tweezers are straight. However, for hard-to-reach spots, you may find tweezers with curved points more helpful. There are also self-closing tweezers, which are useful for painting and holding objects for extended periods.

Tweezers should be handled with care. The tips can be bent if excess pressure is applied. If tweezers fall on a hard surface the tips may be knocked out of alignment. If the damage isn't too severe, the tweezers can be fixed with pliers. However, it is usually advisable to replace the tool.

Needle files. Needle files (the smallest versions are usually called jeweler's files) are available in 4", 5½", and 7" lengths from Excel, General, Mascot Precision Tools, and Micro-Mark. The files, **5**, are offered individually and in sets. They're available with various cross-sections, including flat, half-round, round, oval, square, triangle, and equaling. Needle files are useful for many modeling tasks, including cleaning up metal and plastic parts.

Veteran modelers usually keep two sets of files, one for metal and one for plastic. Metal chips lodged in the files can potentially gouge plastic.

A gentle, smooth motion is all that's necessary when using needle files. Excess side pressure may cause the file to break. To keep the files in tip-top shape, clean them after each. A brass-wire brush run parallel with the file's teeth will clean out debris. Specialty file cleaners are available from Creations Unlimited and Micro-Mark.

Needlenose pliers. Bending wire, installing detail parts, and holding couplers and other small parts are just three of many applications for needle-nose pliers, **6**. They're made by Xuron and others. Made with narrow jaws, they're designed to get into tighter spaces than standard pliers. They are are available in both smooth- and serrated-jaw versions. Smooth-jaw pliers won't mar parts, but they may slip if too much pressure is applied. Serrated-jaw pliers provide a stronger grip.

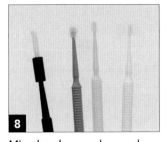

8

Microbrushes can be used for applying paint, glue, or lubricant. Styles include (from left) an ultrabrush, regular, fine, and super fine.

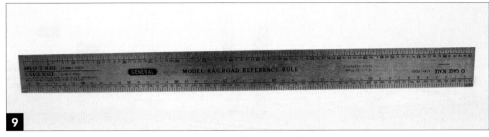

9

A scale rule is an item you can add to your toolbox as you become more experienced in the hobby. The front of the rule has markings for HO, S, and O scales. The reverse features N scale markings and scales in millimeters and 64ths, among other information. Steel rules like this one also serve well as a straightedge when cutting material (such as sheet wood or plastic) with a hobby knife.

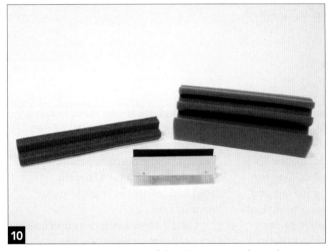

10

Bench cradles hold models safely when you work on them. K.I.S.S. Method Inc. (left rear) and Micro-Mark (right rear) are two companies that produce foam cradles. The cradle in front, sold by Ribbonrail, has an aluminum frame and padded liner.

11

Checking coupler height, wheel gauge, and track spacing are three uses for the National Model Railroad Association (NMRA) standards gauge. It's offered in many popular modeling scales, including HO and N. You can learn more about NMRA standards at www.nmra.org.

Sprue cutters. These flush-cutting tools are designed to safely and cleanly remove plastic parts from molding sprues, **7**. Micro-Mark makes a tweezer-style stainless steel cutter with sharp, thin cutting edges that fits into tight locations for removing small parts. Mascot Precision Tools, Testor, and Xuron offer pliers-style cutters for removing larger parts.

Microbrushes. Microbrushes are some of the most important tools in my toolbox, **8**. Microbrushes can be used to apply paint, liquid adhesive, or lubricant. The disposable brushes feature a head with non-absorbent, non-linting fibers and a flexible handle.

Microbrushes are available with super fine, fine, and regular heads and an ultrabrush (like a paintbrush). Creations Unlimited offers 25- and 40-packs of microbrushes; 100-packs are available from Micro-Mark.

Scale rule. Scale rules are versatile tools, **9**. They include markings for various modeling scales, so they can be used to measure models and detail parts, transfer dimensions from drawings, and compare a model's dimensions to the prototype. Steel versions can be used as a straightedge for cutting.

General and Mascot produce 12" stainless steel scale rules. Both brands have blackened, etched markings in N, HO, S, and O scales. On the reverse, there are scales in millimeters and inches (to 64ths), a reference table for tap and clearance drill sizes for hobby screws, and a table of decimal equivalent for no. 1 through no. 80 drill bits. Others make plastic and steel rules from 6" to 24" long. **Bench**

cradle. A bench cradle will hold models securely and protect them from damage when making repairs, decaling, and painting, **10**. The designs vary among manufacturers. Some feature all-foam construction with or without a compartment for storing tools and parts. Other cradles have an aluminum frame with a padded liner.

Bowser, K.I.S.S. Method, Inc., Micro-Mark, and Ribbonrail all offer work cradles in N and HO scales.

National Model Railroad Association standards gauge. This pocket-sized sheet metal gauge is available for HO and N, as well as many other popular modeling scales, **11**. The tool allows modelers to check coupler height, make sure wheels are properly gauged, and measure track spacing. The standards gauge is available at most well-stocked

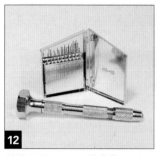

12

A pin vise (manual drill) and bits make it possible to drill small holes in wood, plastic, and soft metal. A case of drill bits, called an index (this one is from Wm. K. Walthers), commonly includes nos. 61 through 80 bits.

13

Quality paintbrushes can handle a variety of painting projects. Brushes with fine tips, like the 20/0 and 10/0 in the foreground, are good for painting figures and detail parts and doing touch-up work. Flex-I-File offers boxed sets with popular brush sizes for large and small jobs.

14

Clear, water-consistency liquid plastic cements are good for plastic-to-plastic joints. A variety of cements are available; they differ in their evaporation times.

hobby shops and directly from the NMRA at www.nmra.org.

Pin vise and drill bits. If you want to add detail parts or body-mounted couplers to locomotives and freight car, you'll need to drill small holes. The best way to do this is with a pin vise and miniature drill bits, **12**. Some modelers consider a pin vise an advanced tool, but it's really not. A pin vise is simply a small, handheld drill designed for use on wood, plastic, and soft metal. Many styles are offered—find one that fits comfortably in your hand.

The drill bits used in a pin vise are small. Bits are numbered: Model railroaders most often use sets including no. 61 (.040") through no. 80 (.0135") bits. In addition, nos. 43, 48, 50, 52, 53, 55, and 56 bits are common for pilot and clearance holes for screws used in truck and coupler installation. Make sure the chuck is completely closed and the bit is centered before you start drilling.

There are a couple of things to remember when using a pin vise and drill bits. First, lubricate the bits with beeswax or bar soap. This will allow the bit to cut through the material faster, and it will extend the life of the bit.

Second, let the bit do the work. Apply just enough pressure to keep the bit in place, and don't bend the bit. Back the bit out of the hole periodically to remove shavings.

Paintbrushes. Touching up paint on models, applying liquid plastic cement, and applying decal setting fluid are just a few uses for paintbrushes, **13**. When purchasing brushes, look for those designed for use with oils and acrylics, as the bristles can withstand the solvents used in hobby paints.

Paintbrushes come in a variety of sizes and shapes (round and flat are most common). Fine-tip brushes (nos. 20/0 through 0) are good for painting detail parts and doing small touch-up work. If you need to paint larger areas, such as window frames on a building, use medium-tip brushes (nos. 1 through 4). These brushes are also good for applying weathering to models using the drybrush technique. Large brushes (nos. 5 through 8) can be used to paint freight cars, buildings, and other items. In addition, large brushes can be used to clean and dust models.

A quality paintbrush that's used correctly, properly cleaned, and stored upright (bristles up) will last several years.

Adhesives. If you walk down the adhesives aisle at the hobby shop, you'll notice there are a variety of glues available for model building. Don't let the options overwhelm you. Each adhesive has a specific use, and knowing the right one to use will save you time, money, and frustration. You'll also be rewarded with models that look

good and have strong, clean bonds.

Except for white glue, all of the adhesives listed here contain volatile solvents and emit fumes that are irritating or harmful. Carefully read and follow the manufacturers' instructions.

Use all adhesives in a well-ventilated area, take frequent breaks, wear personal safety gear, and stay away from ignition sources.

Plastic cement. As the name implies, these solvent-type cements are suitable for plastic-to-plastic joints. The solvent works by melting the top layer of plastic on the adjoining parts, welding them together.

The viscosity (thickness) of plastic cement varies among brands. Clear, watery liquid cements include Tenax 7R, Testor's (no. 3502), Plastruct Bondene and Plastic Weld, Micro-Mark Same Stuff, Squadron Products Plastic Weld, and Tamiya Extra Thin Cement, **14**. Some manufacturers build an application brush into the screw-top bottle cap, but they're often large. A fine paintbrush or Microbrush affords better control and makes it easier to get the glue where you want it.

To use thin liquid cement, dry-fit the parts with a clamp or tape, making sure the joint is tight. Then touch a brush with liquid cement to the joint. The solvent will be pulled into the joint by capillary action. Because the glue

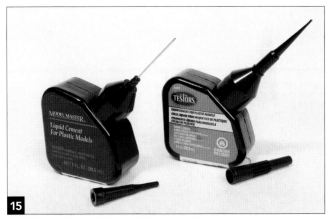

15 The Testor Corp. offers gel-type plastic cements under the Model Master (no. 8872) and Testors (no. 3507) labels. The Model Master version features a fine metal tip, while the Testor Corp. version has a plastic tip.

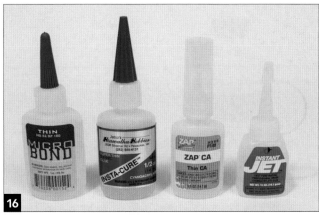

16 Thin cyanoacrylate adhesives (CAs) should be used on tight-fitting joints. Thin CA bonds almost instantly, so parts should be aligned and fitted properly before the adhesive is applied to the joint.

17 Of the three viscosities of CA, medium is the best for general-purpose use. It has a setting time of 5 to 15 seconds, allowing some time for final part positioning. You can put CA on a part, then fit it to the model before it sets.

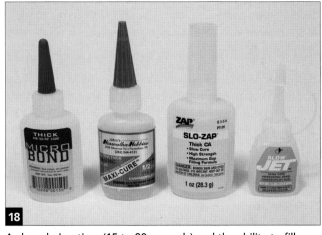

18 A slow drying time (15 to 30 seconds) and the ability to fill gaps are two qualities of thick CA. As the bottles here show, some manufacturers play up the gap-filling qualities of thick CA, while others emphasize the longer working time. Thick CA also works well for reinforcing joints from behind.

etches the plastic, it's best to apply it from behind the joint.

Thick, gel-type plastic cements include Model Master no. 8872 and Testors no. 3507. Both bottles feature built-in needle-point applicators, **15**. To use them, apply a bead of cement to one surface (not so much that it will ooze out of the joint). Gently press the mating parts together and hold for 5-10 seconds. Gels have a longer working time than liquid cements, so there's more time to do final positioning of the parts.

Regardless of the viscosity of the plastic cement used, the mating surfaces should be clean. Use a hobby knife or sandpaper to remove paint from the parts. If you skip this step, the joint will be weak. When used properly, a joint secured with plastic cement will be as strong as the plastic itself.

Plastic cements will keep indefinitely, but liquid cement evaporates quickly if the bottle is left open. If gel cement becomes stringy and thick, it's time to get a new bottle.

Cyanoacrylate adhesive. For bonding dissimilar materials, including metal, wood, resin, and plastic, reach for cyanoacrylate adhesive (CA, or super glue). It comes in different viscosities. The three most often used by model railroaders are thin, medium, and thick.

Thin CA, **16**, is thinner than water. It should only be used on tight joints, such as sides and ends on a freight car.

Similar to liquid plastic cement, apply thin CA to a joint and allow capillary action to draw it in. The CA will bond almost instantly. Brands include Instant Jet, Insta-Cure, Microscale Micro Bond Thin, and Zap CA. Use care, as thin CA can easily flow to unintended locations (including fingers!).

Medium CA, **17**, is ideal for general use. A drop or two on the bottom of an inverted plastic cup or a scrap of styrene is usually sufficient for most projects; a microbrush, piece of wire, or a toothpick make handy glue applicators. Medium CA, sold under the Super Jet, Micro Bond Medium, Insta-Cure+, and Zap-A-Gap Medium CA+ brand names, has a setting time of 5 to 15 seconds.

19

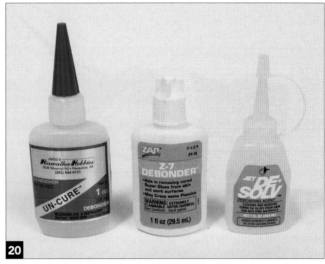

20

Chemical accelerators will speed up the drying time of cyanoacrylate adhesive. However, it may also stain or lift paint, dissolve foam, and craze plastic. Read the label on the bottle or test it on an inconspicuous area before applying accelerator to an entire model.

Cyanoacrylate adhesive will bond skin. If (more accurately, when) this happens, don't panic. Apply debonder to CA and let it dissolve.

Thick CA, **18**, is the slowest drying type of CA, requiring 15 to 30 seconds to set. It's used for filling joints with gaps (some manufacturers call it "gap-filling CA") and bonding large surface areas. Examples include Slow Jet, Maxi-Cure, Micro Bond Thick, and Slo-Zap.

Super glue accelerators, such as Jet Set, Insta-Set, and Zip Kicker, **19**, will cure CA instantly. However, be aware that accelerator may stain or strip some types of paint. While some bottles of

accelerator have a spray adapter, I prefer applying it with a microbrush so I can control the amount being applied and where it's going.

Once opened, a bottle of CA will last about three months. If the adhesive won't hold parts, becomes stringy, or thickens, throw it away and get a new bottle. Keep CA in a dry, cool place.

It's pretty much a given that you'll have to unclog the tip of a CA bottle at some point in your modeling career. Many people (myself included) have

used pushpins to remedy this problem. Unfortunately, this is a temporary fix. The pin just pushes the clog back into the bottle, and it will likely plug the tip again. A better solution is to clear the clog with a drill bit.

While CA is handy, it has some drawbacks. The fumes from CA can fog clear window glazing. This can be prevented by dipping the clear parts in Pledge Future floor polish prior to installation. The vapors also have the potential of fogging plated parts, like those found on the sides on locomotives and passenger cars.

Cyanoacrylate adhesive will also bond skin instantly. If this happens to you, don't try to pull the skin apart. Instead, apply debonder, **20**, or nail polish remover with acetone and let the adhesive dissolve.

White glue. It's not just for school any more. White glue, **21**, is a synthetic polyvinyl acetate emulsion that's useful for porous materials such as paper, plaster, wood, cardstock, and cardboard. Probably the best-known brand is Elmer's Glue-All.

White glue can be applied full strength or diluted with water. However, thinned glue loses a great deal of strength. It should only be diluted in situations where you need the glue to soak in. White glue dries clear and can be cleaned up with water.

21

22

You may have thought white glue was a distant memory from your grade school days. However, the water-soluble glue has many modeling applications, such as bonding porous materials (paper, wood, and plaster) and securing scenery.

Wood glue, like white glue, can be used on porous materials. Also known as aliphatic resin or carpenter's glue, wood glue has a stronger bond than white glue when fully cured.

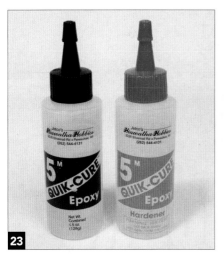

23

Two-part epoxy is a good choice for non-porous items like plastic, resin, and metal. It consists of epoxy and hardener that need to be mixed in equal parts before being applied. The five-minute variety is most common.

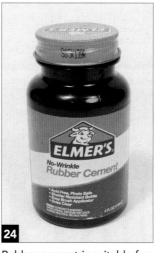

24

Rubber cement is suitable for attaching signs to billboards or structures. Apply a thin coat on the two gluing surfaces, let it set until it isn't tacky, and press the pieces together.

25

Heavy-duty contact cement (left) is designed for gluing large pieces of non-porous material. The cement creates an almost instant bond, giving you only one chance to align the parts. Goo (middle) is a rubber-based contact cement. Gorilla Glue (right) is a heavy-duty polyurethane adhesive.

Wood (carpenter's) glue. This is an aliphatic resin adhesive, **22**. As you probably guessed by the name, carpenter's glue is suitable for wood. It can also be used on paper and other porous materials, but be aware that unlike white glue, it doesn't dry clear.

A note of caution about wood and white glues: If you plan on staining wood (such as the bents on a trestle), do so prior to gluing the parts. Any glue that oozes out of a joint will seal the wood, preventing the stain from soaking in.

Wood glue yields a stronger bond than white glue. It requires 10 to 40 minutes to set and 24 hours to cure. Wood glue is made by Elmer's and several other manufacturers.

Epoxy. This two-part adhesive is designed for securing plastic, resin, metal, glass, and other non-porous materials, **23**. Five-minute epoxy is commonly used by modelers. It consists of epoxy and hardener that need to be mixed thoroughly in equal parts before application.

Epoxy was widely used in the days before CA as it was one of few adhesives that could bond dissimilar materials. Today epoxy is used to secure weights inside freight cars and reinforce joints initially bonded

with CA. Modelers also use epoxy in situations where longer working times and higher shear strength are desired. Epoxy dries clear and glossy.

Contact cement. There are two types of contact cement. The first is rubber cement, **24**. It's good for attaching signs to billboards or structures. Just put a thin coat on each mating surface, let the glue set until it isn't tacky, and press the parts together.

If you need to bond large pieces of cardstock, metal, paper, and other non-porous materials, try heavy-duty contact cement, **25**. The liquid adhesive is applied to both surfaces and allowed to partially set. The parts are then pressed together. Contact cement creates an almost instant bond, so make sure the parts are aligned correctly the first time.

Use heavy-duty contact cement with caution as the solvents in it can damage styrene. Brand names include Walthers Goo, DAP Weldwood Contact Cement, Barge Cement, and Pliobond, among others.

Heavy-duty polyurethane glue, such as Gorilla Glue, is a good general adhesive where great strength is needed.

Pressure-sensitive adhesive. Micro-Mark's Liquid PSA and Woodland Scenics' Scenic Accents Glue are exam-

26

Pressure-sensitive adhesive can be used for positioning figures, applying window glazing, and securing plastic handrails. The glue, which is compatible with wood, plastic, and metal, is white straight from the bottle but turns clear and tacky.

ples of pressure-sensitive adhesive, **26**. These comes out of the bottle white but dries tacky and clear. Among its many uses are positioning figures securing glazing in locomotives or cabooses.

Since pressure-sensitive adhesive stays tacky, figures and parts can be repositioned. The adhesive, which is compatible with plastic, wood, and metal, can be washed off with water until it turns clear and tacky.

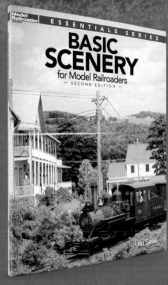

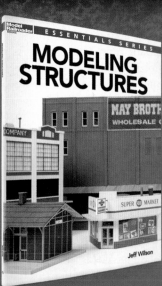